Alec Motyer has had a profo
my preaching. In this book he p
expository preaching at the reader
and Biblically solid a book on prea

Tim Keller
Senior Pastor, Redeemer Presbyterian Church, New York City

Alec Motyer once said of Allan Harman's commentary on Isaiah, 'His work has made me wish wholeheartedly that I could start all over again.' And Alec's succinct and stirring treatise on preaching makes me wish wholeheartedly that I could start all over again— in that blessed privilege of preaching, praying and pastoring.

Dale Ralph Davis
Well-respected author and Bible expositor, rural Tennessee

Alec Motyer is a man of the Bible. His love and understanding for the Scriptures, that was instilled in him from a very young age spills out in his writings and also in his recent book, *Preaching? Simple Teaching on Simply Preaching*. Alec has done a fantastic job in making preaching as simple as the title suggests. The main point that stands out throughout the book is that preaching is uncomplicated, but requires work, and hard work. The work is not only in the preparation, but also the behaviour and the spirituality of the preacher.

I liked the comparison of a sermon to baking a cake. He suggests that just as we would not put the cake ingredients in front of our guests, but rather put them together orderly and fashionably, then we should do the same with the sermon. A sermon is more than just its ingredients. Another of his sayings is that sermon preparation is one part inspiration, and nine parts perspiration.

The book is very helpful to both the novice as well as the veteran preacher. I highly recommend the book.

David Zadok
Director, Christian Witness to Israel, Hagefen Publishing, Israel

One of our best loved preacher-theologians, Alec Motyer, applies his customary wisdom, wit and clarity to provide a practical but inspiring introduction to the task of preaching. This refreshing guide, laced with excellent Biblical examples and astute observations from personal experience, will be a great read for preachers old and new, and I warmly commend it.

Jonathan Lamb
Director, Langham Preaching, Oxford

Given the content, readability and insights which Alec Motyer's book contains and the primacy of preaching combined with the present day abdication of confidence in the divinely ordained instrumentality of faithful expository public preaching of God's Word, this book is a "must" for preachers and for those who want to understand preaching and encourage preachers.

Harry L. Reeder
Pastor of Preaching and Leadership, Briarwood Presbyterian Church
Birmingham, Alabama

ALEC MOTYER

PREACHING?

Simple Teaching on Simply Preaching

CHRISTIAN
FOCUS

Copyright © Alec Motyer 2013

paperback ISBN 978-1-78191-130-3
epub ISBN 978-1-78191-266-9
Mobi ISBN 978-1-78191-267-6

10 9 8 7 6 5 4 3 2 1

Published in 2013
Reprinted in 2013
by
Christian Focus Publications Ltd,
Geanies House, Fearn,
Ross-shire, IV20 1TW, Scotland.
www.christianfocus.com

Cover design
by
Daniel van Straaten

Printed by
Bell and Bain, Glasgow

MIX
Paper from
responsible sources
FSC® C007785

CONTENTS

Chapter 1

Between You and Me

The memory is still very fresh, and still fills me with the same feeling of heart-stopping anxiety. I was at the beginning of full-time ministry, faced, as was then common even for assistants, with the task of preaching at least once on Sundays and often at the mid week prayer and Bible study meeting as well. I had done quite a bit of speaking previously, and I had looked forward to the preaching side of ministry. Indeed, from the start I knew that this was the very heart of the work of the Christian minister. But I had no idea how to go about it. Sermons and talks were things that 'just came', and, indeed, so it had been in my case. Usually I had been invited to speak on a subject or, for whatever reason, a subject had proposed itself, and thoughts began, usually slowly, sometimes laboriously, to gather around the theme. But that seemed no longer the case, and the old experience of thoughts gathering and forming no longer seemed to work. Saturday evenings were anticipated with increasing foreboding. If confession is good for the soul, I recall one occasion when, by 5:30 p.m. on Sunday nothing had yet 'come', and the 6:30 deadline gave me something of the feeling of a Great War trench awaiting the whistle to go over the top.

Looking back, it took me a surprisingly long time to learn that sermons are not spontaneous or extended intuitions but things to be worked at, and it took even longer to discover how to go about it.

My discoveries along these lines are not, I think, earth-shaking, and, I expect, in no sense novel. I recall my aunts reading aloud the inset in the church magazine with its regular feature of Household Tips – Monday's Washing, Tuesday's Sewing ... and the scorn they heaped, monthly, on the contributor! 'Picture putting that in! That's an old remedy! I remember Grandmother doing that!' You may and probably will pour like scorn on me, but I mean well. I have a feeling that if there are any sitting on Saturday evening looking agonizingly at their Bibles, waiting for the golden words to spring from the page, then I have good news for them.

Don't sit and stare. There's work to be done, and here is one way to go about it.

Chapter 2

Work to be done: the Pursuit

Not everyone can be what people call a 'good preacher', but no one need be a 'bad preacher'. That is one of the convictions which drive this little book! When I remarked on what a poor showing a local bishop made on a recent visit, my companion said, 'Of course, our bishop is not a preacher.' Maybe not, but he should be! It's what he spends a great deal of his time doing, but, dear, good man, he had fallen into the mistake of thinking that being a 'good preacher' was a matter of 'gift' and either you have it or you don't, and if you don't there's nothing you can do about it. Not so! No, indeed!

What makes a sermon 'bad'?
I am going to venture an opinion here. See if it matches your experience. The majority of (if not, to a degree, all) 'bad'

sermons are 'bad' because they are muddled. An elderly lady, much prized in our circle, possessed a remarkably loud whisper, and one Sunday evening during the sermon she whispered to her daughter, inadvertently addressing the whole church; 'What's he talking about? Is he never going to stop?' Your heart goes out to her, doesn't it? You've been there too, as, indeed I have. But the point is this: muddle is something that can be sorted out. Some people have a natural capacity for setting a subject out, and there is never any doubt what they have said, or why they have moved on to the next aspect of their subject. And in the end it is all a clear, rounded whole. Their minds work in distinct 'points' with precise subdivisions. For most of us that sort of thing is a matter of hard work and detailed preparation. That is exactly my point. 'Good' preaching, in the sense of being plain and unmistakable in the pulpit, is something that can be achieved. Once we have seen it as a target to aim at, it becomes a target we can hit, a step in the right direction to being an acceptable preacher.

Sermons and Essays

And here's something else to consider. Another sort of sermon which 'loses' its listeners is the written essay more or less read out in the pulpit. My first senior minister used to take a fully written manuscript into the pulpit, because, as he would say, without it he became 'diffuse'. But his largish Bible also served him as a sort of interim filing system, an 'in-tray' of letters to be answered, book references to be looked up, helpful cuttings, jottings for future use – amounting to quite a large bulk of extraneous material. Another addition would not be noticed, nor indeed its absence missed! On two occasions he got into the pulpit and, leaf as he would through his Bible, the vital pages were still at home, not there amongst the almost archaeological layers of interleaving! Diffuse or not, he turned out to be a much better preacher!

We will return to this matter later, but the point is this: unlike the muddled, or 'ball-of-wool', sermon, the essay-sermon is very well prepared indeed, and very orderly, but it is of the essence of an essay to pass imperceptibly from one point to the next. We were taught at school to end each paragraph of our essays in such a way that it prepared for the next paragraph. This made for a coherent flow of thought – on paper (where an essay belongs) – but as a spoken exercise it leaves the hearer behind, wondering, How did we get here? For preaching is a speaker-hearer relationship, and the preacher has to learn to give the hearer space to listen. A man said to his fast-talking minister: 'Vicar, you must learn to go more slowly. I am a slow listener.' Up to a point we all are slow listeners! In a sermon there have to be pauses, repetitions. Movement from one aspect of the topic to the next has to be 'flagged up'. The essay type of preaching can, then, for the hearer, fall into the category of the muddled. But, again, this is a matter which will concern us in more detail later on.

How to think of a Sermon

A sermon is like baking a cake. There is, first of all, the objective. It is a madeira cake, or a sponge cake or a fruit cake – or whatever. Then there is the gathering of all the ingredients – not any old ingredients but the ingredients essential to producing that particular cake. You need fruit for a fruit cake but it would be out of place for a plain madeira cake. You need jam for a sponge cake but not for a currant scone. And finally the ingredients have to be put together in the proper order – look at any cookery book and you will see this insistence on proper order: it is the section headed 'Method', how to put the ingredients together. Should we pursue the illustration further? The period in the oven is you in your study, sweating over the huge responsibility that is yours!

But, enough! A sermon is also like dressing a shop window. When we first lived in a remote village, the window of the village shop was just an extension of the stockroom. Everything the shop had on offer was there! In fact, there was so much in the window that no one ever bothered looking in it; there was so much to see that the passer-by saw nothing. Contrast window dressers who know their business! They put into the window what they are, at that moment, setting out to sell, and if they include other things besides (so that the window has an eye-catching variety) they position them in such a way as to lead the eye step by step to the central feature. Sermons are equally selective. Maybe we would not wish to put it this way, but a really important question is 'What are we intending to sell?' Bible in hand, we have a stockroom full of the most amazing collection of goods to offer – real bargains too! So what shall we put in the window this Sunday morning or evening, this Wednesday 'mid-week sabbath'? Everything must lead the eye to that central truth. There must be no doubt what is on offer. The extraordinary Calvin Coolidge, the silent, or at the most, monosyllabic President of the United States, returning from church, was asked by his wife what the sermon was about. He replied, 'Sin.' 'Well,' urged Mrs Coolidge, 'what did he say about it?' 'He was against it,' said the President.

Hmm. Well ... yes! But the sermon had made its point, hadn't it? The product for sale was unmistakable, and, to say the least, it had been taken home on appro.

There is no more arduous task!

I must beware of making personal experience into a universal truth. The fact is that I find sermon preparation such hard work that I actively 'back off' from starting! Sure, this is not true of everyone. There must be those to whom sermons come more easily. I hope so, but I have a feeling (though it may be no more than a reflection of personal experience) that if preachers are not finding sermon preparation hard work they are not giving their sermons a fair crack of the whip. Of course there are other sides of the picture: it is a privilege of privileges to be driven to such involvement in the Word of God, to be required to buckle down to the precious Scriptures. Yes indeed, but it is also demanding, frequently burdensome, rarely easy – and always, in the event, endlessly delightful! One part inspiration, nine parts perspiration.

Chapter 3

The Heart of the Matter

I hope you are convinced that the Bible is the Word of God, and that the task of the preacher is, as we have just said, to get deeply involved in that Word, the Holy Scriptures, and preach it. This book, at any rate, rests on that conviction.

Jesus, Head over all things to the Church
The supreme kingship of the Lord Jesus Christ must ever be our most sensitive concern, and nothing must usurp His authority. The reason for pointing this out is that those who exalt the Bible to its proper place and high dignity are not infrequently accused of 'bibliolatry', putting the Bible in the place of Jesus. Not so! Rather we exalt the Bible *because* we want to give Jesus His place 'high over all', and we exalt the preaching of the Bible because, in principle,

this is the way to make Him known, and it is He who has commanded us to do so.

No Christian finds difficulty with Matthew's portrayal of the Risen Lord. Matthew operates with a narrow focus – to get us without delay from the empty tomb (28:6) to Galilee (28:10, 16) where we will hear Jesus proclaim that 'all authority ... in heaven and earth' belongs to Him (28:18, NKJV). In this way, Matthew voiced the common testimony of all who profess the name of Christ: He is Lord; all authority is His. But Matthew, in leaving it at that, fails to answer a vital question: how does our Lord exercise this authority? How does He make His authoritative will known to His earthly people? How does the Lord exercise Lordship?

In the marvellously dovetailing testimony of the four Gospels, it is left for Luke to take up where Matthew left off. With Luke, we join the pair (surely husband and wife?) who walked to Emmaus (24:13). Their story is of fundamental significance: they were barred from seeing Jesus in His risen glory until they had first seen Him in the Scriptures (24:25-27, 31, 32). Furthermore, under Luke's guidance, we are privileged, next, to enter the upper room. Jesus comes (24:36), and when He has, at last, convinced His gathered disciples that it is indeed He, Luke tells us (24:45) that He 'opened their understanding, that they might comprehend the Scriptures' and He said 'thus it is written ... that repentance and remission of sins should be preached'. The significance of these events is clear: we can neither know the risen Lord, nor know how and what to preach about Him to the world except through the Scriptures. They are both our teacher and our task; our education and our message. Note, in particular, the sequence: the risen Lord, the written Scriptures, the command to preach. If we are to be faithful to Him, the risen, exalted, supreme, authoritative Lord Jesus Christ, then we are to be Bible people and preaching people. This is all the authority and direction we need!

Peter's Retrospect: God's fourfold Choice

But to move on. In Acts the entrance of Gentiles into the Church was a matter of controversy – whether they should be there at all, and, if so, on what terms. At the Council of Jerusalem (Acts 15:7) Peter contributed a lesson from Church history. He believed that what he said was common knowledge and commonly agreed: 'You know that a good while ago (lit., 'from original/primitive days') God chose ... that by my mouth the Gentiles should hear the word of the gospel and believe.'

Have a go at analysing that verse. God, said Peter, made a fourfold choice: he chose *preaching* ('by my mouth'), *hearers* ('the Gentiles'), the *subject matter* ('the gospel'), and the *result* ('and believe'). It is an extraordinarily full statement in such a few words. Look at it. The Church grows by preaching; the preaching reaches those God intends; its content is the gospel; and the result is responsive faith. All chosen by God: *His* will, *His* method, *His* message, *His* results.

In the late 1960s the local clergy where I was working seemed to be gripped by an enthusiasm for closing churches! We had inherited far too many buildings, they urged. There were far too many empty seats on any given Sunday, they used to say, ignoring the fact that since those churches were built the population of that area had increased maybe a hundredfold! It was a real spirit of defeatism and retrenchment – though usually cloaked under the heading of 'slimming down for advance'. Every time a church fell vacant, they affirmed, it should at once be closed! But, to the great indignation of the church closers, when St X fell vacant the authorities – in Anglican terms, the 'patrons' – got in first, and made a new appointment, and, adding insult to injury, under its new minister St X bucked the trend, and began to grow in every department – Sunday congregations, Sunday schools, youth work, the elderlies, the lot! Indignation overflowed! 'Perhaps Mr Y would be kind enough to tell us, at our next meeting, how he has managed all this!' Dear Mr Y could not but agree, but, as he left he whispered to me: 'Is it enough to tell them that it is all a matter of praying and preaching?' But that's it. God's method of church growth is preaching the Word, watered by believing prayer.

Acts, a Manual for Church Growth

Here is a principle to ponder: that which makes the Church a distinctive company in the world is the Word of God – or, putting it more concisely, the Word of God is the constitutive reality at the heart of the Church. It is what makes the Church what it is, and it has always been so. What, for example, made Noah and his family a distinctive, separate entity in the world? Hebrews 11:7 says Noah was 'divinely warned' (*chrymatistheis*, 'having had a revelation imparted to him'), and was 'moved with godly fear' (*eulabytheis*, 'urged on by spiritual sensitivity'). Likewise, Abraham was one to whom the Lord spoke (Gen. 12:1; 17:1); 'the word of the LORD came to Abram' (15:1). That is what marked him out. As soon as Israel had emerged from the isolation of the wilderness years to become a nation among the nations, they were meant to excite this admiration from the watching world: 'What great nation is there that has such statutes …' (Deut. 4:8), i.e., their distinctiveness was that they possessed the Word of God. Over the centuries the volume of inherited revealed truth increased until, for us, it has become the completed Bible, and just as we can look back and say that our forebears – right back to Adam (e.g. Gen. 2:16, 17) – were people of the Word, so we, their inheritors, are people of the Book.

What we call 'the Acts of the Apostles' is a case in point. In its twenty-eight chapters there are about thirty-seven references to the growth of the Church. Indeed 'The Growing Church' would be a more suitable title than 'the Acts of the Apostles'. Of the thirty-seven or so references, six associate growth with the quality of church life and of Christian character, seven link growth with the evidence of 'signs and wonders', and twenty-four link growth with the preaching of the Word of God – indeed in 12:24 the growth of the Church is actually called the growth of the Word, as if they were so closely related that they could be identified one with the other.

The Day of Pentecost

In Acts 1 the Church is 'under starter's orders'; in Acts 2 the Starter's gun is fired. The promise of Acts 1:5 is fulfilled, and the programme of Acts 1:8 is set in train. The vital topic of Bible analysis will concern us later, but here is a preliminary example, an analytical survey of Acts 2:2-4, the four things the Holy Spirit did on the Day of Pentecost:

- 'Filled the whole house' (v. 2). The Holy Spirit came first to the place where His people were. This is the fulfilment of what Jesus spoke of in John 7:37-39 (cf., John 16:7): the New Testament full flood of the Holy Spirit, flowing from Jesus, granted to believers. In an act just as 'once for all' as the work of Jesus on the Cross, the Holy Spirit came into the world: He is now everywhere we are.

- 'Sat upon each of them' (v. 3). This represents what other Scriptures call the indwelling of the Holy Spirit in each believer; or what is spoken of as the 'seal' and 'guarantee' ('down payment', or 'deposit') of the Spirit (Eph. 1:13, 14), the 'baptism' promised in Acts 1:5.

- 'Filled with the Spirit' describes some special enduement with the Holy Spirit granted for a particular time and task – just as Peter was 'filled' with the Spirit on two subsequent recorded occasions, enabling him to meet special needs at a special time (Acts 4:8, 31). This corresponds to the 'episodic' filling with the Spirit experienced in the Old Testament (e.g., Judg. 6:34), and represents, for us, the readiness of the Holy Spirit to leap to our aid.

- 'Speak with other tongues' is the particular 'gift' of the Spirit granted on the Day of Pentecost, the gift of intelligible communication ('everyone heard them speak in his own language', 2:6) of 'the wonderful works of God' (v. 11).

On the Day of Pentecost the Holy Spirit clothed Himself in visible form, and His choice of 'tongues' established the special focus of the day: He came with the particular purpose of making the Church a speaking church (John 15:26-27), a communicating body, and Peter takes this theme up in his quotation from Joel 2:28-32. The outpouring of the Spirit is given for the particular purpose of creating 'prophets' – sons and daughters, menservants and maidservants all alike recipients of the Spirit and gifted for prophecy – that they too may speak intelligibly to the world the 'wonderful works of God'.

Paul's Prospectus

'Preaching' – in its broad sense of telling the good news of Jesus, and in its narrower sense of individual, formal proclamation – is a point, then, at which many lines of New Testament testimony converge. Let Paul add his word. With 2 Timothy we come to one of the most important moments – and documents – of the New Testament. This lovely little letter sits on the significant dividing line between the apostolic and the post-apostolic church (2 Tim. 4:6-8), and in it Paul offers Timothy (and us) a prospectus for the days ahead. It is surely telling that he does not define the Church of the post-apostolic future in terms of an 'apostolic succession' of people holding this or that office in the Church, nor, indeed, does he see the future marked by ongoing and fresh revelations of divine truth through the Holy Spirit. Indeed, the one unmistakable reference to the Holy Spirit in 2 Timothy points to Him as the Guardian of truth already possessed (1:14). This is the hallmark of Paul's thinking as he commits the future to Timothy. The Church is not a body in pursuit of the truth, but already possessing it (1:13), and called to share it:

• Timothy's task is to lay hold of the power of the Holy Spirit to 'hold fast' what he already possesses (1:13, 14).

- His duty is to work at the Word of Truth (2:15).

- This Word of Truth is both the inherited 'sacred writings' – i.e., what we call the Old Testament – (3:15), along with the apostolic teaching – i.e., the New Testament – (3:10, 14), which, together, form 'all Scripture ... given by inspiration of God' (3:16), sufficient for perfecting 'the man of God' (3:17).

- Timothy's task, in the light of coming judgment and the coming of the Lord Jesus (4:1) is to 'preach the Word' (4:2).

What a simple, compelling prospectus! What a satisfying, attractive and assuredly fruitful task! What a manageable calling! What a privilege – to inherit, possess, guard and absorb oneself in and preach what God has 'breathed out': His Word, our education to maturity, our message to the world! That, in a word, is what the Church is 'all about'. This is the single point where so much of the New Testament converges. God's purpose for His people is proclamation.

Chapter 4

Faithful Teachers

The New Testament has an enormous vocabulary in connection with communicating the gospel. I started years ago to try to collect what the New Testament says about 'preaching' – in the broadest sense of any and every way in which we try to share the good news. I started by dedicating one page in my file to 'vocabulary', thinking that would surely be enough. At the moment, my collected items fill three fat files, of which vocabulary takes up one whole file all to itself! It is interesting that the most frequently used verbs are the simple verbs of 'saying' or 'speaking', like Paul writes in 1 Thessalonians 2:16, 'forbidding us to speak to the Gentiles that they may be saved'. Making Jesus the topic of conversation is not a thing that requires anyone to write a book about! It is an essentially simple matter, matching, indeed, the simplicity of the gospel itself.

Key Words

But elsewhere Paul sails in deeper waters. Writing to Timothy (2 Tim. 1:11), he speaks of himself as 'a preacher, an apostle, and a teacher'. His apostleship, of course, was his unique, unrepeatable status and authority, unavailable to us as such, but available to us to copy if we are to be apostolic Christians. This unique apostolicity, as we saw in 2 Timothy, is continued in the Church by the possession, dominance, authority and proclamation of the Word of God. Paul also called himself a 'preacher'. Here the word is *kyrux*, which expresses an important idea. It is a 'town-crier' word, still in evidence in (usually) rural settings which wish to recapture the romance of the past. Ask this bellowing, bell-ringing fellow, in all his fancy dress, why he is making such a din, and he will reply, pointing to the Town Hall, 'They told me!' And also ask why is he shouting these particular words, and the reply will be the same; 'They told me!' The essential mark of the *kyrux* ('herald') is not noise but faithfulness to a message given by a superior authority. The *kyrux* does not make up what he says; he is not sharing his own best thought for the day; he is not a person of 'ifs' and 'maybes'. He is a 'man under authority', saying what he heard elsewhere, doing what he was told to do, faithful to a given message and task, and determined that all shall hear (cf., Rom. 10:14, 15, 17; 2 Tim. 4:17).

Thirdly, Paul described himself as a 'teacher' (*didaskalos*), and in doing so he opened up a central New Testament truth about 'preaching'. The verb (*didasko*, to teach) and the nouns *didaskalia*, the function of teaching, and *didache*, the body of truth taught, are widely used and fundamentally important. As in a classroom lesson, in each sermon:

- there is a central truth to be conveyed

- there is a planned method of setting that truth out

- there is a determination to bring that truth home with clarity, understanding, application and acceptability to the hearers.

No teachers worth their salt leave their classes in any doubt of what a particular lesson is about; they come with a prepared presentation, each point designed to make some facet of the central truth shine clearly, and to build up, step by step, to a total presentation. Clarity is the order of the day; the presentation of truth the great objective. This is exactly true of the Christian preacher also! Not, of course, that sharing the gospel allows us to adopt a detached stance such as the words 'teacher' and 'teaching' could of themselves suggest. Certainly not! It would be worth your while to look up 'to teach' in a concordance and to note the words with which it is connected – like, for example, Colossians 3:16 says 'teaching and admonishing', where the latter word means something akin to our use of 'counselling' (*noutheteo*), the gentle application of the message; or 1 Timothy 6:2, 'teach and exhort', where the second word (*parakaleo*) always, as here, tends to include the warmth of 'encouraging' alongside clarity of exhortation. We have all listened to preachers who, we felt, were more interested in blacking eyes than in comforting hearts and tenderly directing lives. In such a way the truth may be 'bulldozed' in, but it is not New Testament 'teaching'.

Living in the True Succession: Going back to Basics

Always keeping in mind, then, that Paul, 'serving the Lord
… with many tears … taught publicly and from house to
house' (Acts 20:19-20), we need to remind ourselves also
that he chose the office of teaching as the succession
he desired to see in the post-apostolic Church. Timothy
was instructed to take the truth he had inherited and
to commit it 'to faithful men who will be able (*hikanos*,
'competent') to teach (*didasko*) others also' (2 Tim. 2:2).

But we can move to even higher ground: the Lord Jesus
would have concurred with this emphasis on 'teaching'.
The introduction to The Sermon on the Mount is
impressively spacious: 'when he was seated his disciples
came to him, and he opened his mouth and taught them'
(Matt. 5:1, 2). And when the Sermon was finished we
read that 'the people were astonished at his teaching, for
he taught them as one having authority' (Matt. 7:28-29).
It was His intention to teach, and His hearers recognized
what He was doing. Take another example which
underlines a different aspect of the same thing: when Jesus
completed the series of seven parables in Matthew 13, He
faced His disciples with an unexpected question: 'Have
you understood all these things?' (13:51). He did not ask
'Did you enjoy the parables?' – a question addressed to
the emotions or the heart; nor did He ask 'What do you
propose to do by way of response?' – a question addressed
to the will; but 'Have you understood?' – a question
to the mind. Have you grasped the truth? Have you
been instructed?– I have been teaching; have you been
learning? But the Lord's question should not surprise
us. It reflects something He has stressed all through this
passage. The seed of the Word is snatched away by 'the

wicked one' where there is no understanding (13:19). By contrast, the good ground 'is he who hears the word and understands it' (13:23). The mind has been addressed and instructed, and the truth has been grasped. The seed remains the same; it is ever fertile, but in the one case there is no fruitfulness and in the other there is fruitage up to 100 per cent, because in the one case there was no understanding and in the other the truth was understood, the mind engaged and instructed.

The Crucial Difference

Put it this way: what makes the difference between a converted and an unconverted person? Ephesians 4:17-24 gives the answer (though indeed it is widespread in the New Testament, cf., Rom. 1:18-19, 21, 25; 1 Pet. 1:13, 18, 22): 'Gentiles walk in the futility of their mind, having their understanding darkened', whereas Christians have 'learned Christ ... been taught by him, as the truth is in Jesus'. The mind has been addressed; the truth has been grasped. Other passages need to be considered, of course, if we are to fill out this picture, but Ephesians 4 insists on the fundamental need to grasp 'truth in Jesus'. So, let us again take the highest ground and watch Jesus Himself at work. In Luke 24 the risen Lord walks with two on the Emmaus road. He refuses to allow them to recognize Him (v. 16) though that would have been sufficient to solve their problem. Instead, He began with Moses and all the prophets and 'expounded (*diermyneuo*, 'to interpret') to them in all the Scriptures the things concerning himself' (v. 27). Their reaction is illuminating: '"Did not our heart burn within us while he talked with us on the road, and while he opened the Scriptures to us?" So they arose ...

and returned to Jerusalem ... and told ...' (vv. 32-35). Note the order of events: the mind was instructed, the heart burned, the feet were turned in a different direction, and the mouth was opened! That's the biblical sequence: through the mind to the heart, and on to a changed life and the word of testimony. All the things we would desire to result from our preaching! And they all arise from the mind that has grasped scriptural truth.

This may sound a bit of a 'high-flown' way to say it, but what we have seen in Luke 24 is a piece of 'biblical psychology'. The instructed mind is the foundation of the work of God in us. It is when the mind embraces with clarity what the Bible teaches that the heart is warmed, the will mobilized, the life redirected and the tongue loosed. This is not to say that as preachers we should never address the emotions, exhort the will or help our hearers to speak for Jesus. In 2 Timothy 4:2 Paul directs Timothy to 'convince, rebuke, exhort'. 'Rebuke' (*epitimao*, 'to censure, warn') is addressed to the conscience, calling for reformation of behaviour that has gone astray; 'exhort' (*parakaleo*, 'to beseech, exhort, encourage') is addressed to the will, a concern to promote right conduct. But 'convince' addresses the mind, and that comes first. Furthermore, after the three commands Paul adds a description of the context in which they are all alike to be executed: 'with all patience and teaching'. In other words, Paul knew biblical psychology, and we who preach must learn his ways.

Chapter 5

'This Came Out'

The world is full of long words, and 'exposition' is one of them. I remember Dr J. I. Packer once giving a tongue-in-cheek definition of what 'exposition' means – an exposition must deal with more than one verse, be at least an hour and ten minutes long, with the first twenty minutes spent reminding the hearers what was said last week. It was a fair caricature for the time. The great and unique Dr Martyn Lloyd-Jones was at the height of his God-given powers, hugely and deservedly influential, a magnificent expository preacher: therefore, 'exposition' must be 'what the Doctor did' week by week! It would, of course, have been more accurate to say exposition is what the Doctor would have ordered! And he certainly would have insisted that 'My way is my way; you must find your way'. For preaching is a very personal and individual exercise. We can learn from each other, but must not copy each other. It won't work! Like criminals we must each discover our own modus operandi – find out what is our own brand of murder – and, hopefully, get away with it!

'This ... came out'

The sad inadequacy of Aaron as a replacement for Moses – albeit temporary – shines out in the perfectly ludicrous excuse he gave for making the golden calf: 'I cast (the gold) into the fire and this calf came out' (Exod. 32:24). We find ourselves prompted to expostulate, 'Did you ever!' Though, mind you, an angry Moses would be enough to make any of us lose our wits! However, what Aaron said so foolishly encapsulates what we are all trying to do in the hot furnace of sermon preparation: we are on the watch for 'what comes out'. That is, indeed, what 'exposition' means. It is what an expository sermon is.

Exposition is the restatement of a Scripture – whether a word, a verse, a chapter or a book – so that its message emerges with clarity.

Limited Aim

There is a limitation of aim: to bring out what is there; to restate. The opposite of 'exposition' is 'importation'. Take, for example, the idea of 'fleeing from God' in Psalm 139:7. I have heard more than one sermon which turned the idea of 'fleeing' into a question: Why should a person want to flee from God? The usual answer was 'because of sin'. The sinner senses not only personal unfitness to stand before God, but also the eternal danger involved in doing so. Therefore the need for flight. A different answer touches on those times when, like Jonah, we find the will of God distasteful, too difficult, unacceptable or impossible, and 'flee to Tarshish from the presence of the Lord' (Jonah 1:3). Now both of these are scriptural truths: the mere presence of the Lord is, in fact, the sinner's eternal danger; the call of God is often the moment of resistance – 'Here am I! Send my sister!' But neither thought arises from or is found in Psalm 139! In other words, they are, as far as Psalm 139 is concerned, importations, however valid they are in their own right. Psalm 139 is obsessed with the bliss of not being able to escape the presence of this marvellous and omnipotent God. He is in front and behind us; His hand is over us and His wings under us. No escape and no regrets!

The power of an expository ministry arises from bringing out what is there. The seed is the Word of God (Luke 8:11); the fertility is in the seed. The preacher's task is to get the seed out of the packet and into the good soil of instructed, understanding minds (Matt. 13:23).

Going Paul's Way

Acts 17:2-4 allows us to watch a master at work. Paul's own view of the situation was that, though he had suffered arrogant violence (*hubristhentes*) at Philippi, he was nevertheless 'bold in our God to speak to you the gospel of God' (1 Thess. 2:2). So what did he actually do? 'For three Sabbaths (he) reasoned with them from the Scriptures, explaining and demonstrating ...' 'Reasoned' (*dialegomai*) is a good rendering. In its New Testament examples it means 'to argue a case' – not 'to argue' in the sense of violent disagreement, dispute or controversy, but in the sense of presenting and supporting a point of view with the aim of winning the other person over. (See Acts 18:4

and 19:8 where it is linked with 'persuading'.) It is mistake to reduce *dialegomai* to a bland meaning like 'discuss'. It is much more specific: it means 'making out a case', marshalling and presenting evidence as compellingly as possible. It accords with what we noted above about the priority of the mind and understanding.

The remaining two verbs in Acts 17:2-4 are equally instructive. What NKJV renders 'explaining' is, literally, 'opening' (as AV, RV). It is used of opening deaf ears (Mark 7:34), blinkered eyes (Luke 24:31), and, beautifully, of the Lord opening the heart (Acts. 16:14). In Luke 24 the Lord not only opened eyes and minds (v. 45) but also 'opened the Scriptures' (v. 32). What a vivid description of making the Word of God plain! It is Isaiah's sealed book all over again (Isa. 29:11-12) – and what an experience on the Emmaus road when He who is the great subject of all the Scriptures 'explained to them in all the Scriptures the things concerning himself'! It must indeed have been like opening the door into a well-lit but hitherto unexplored treasure store. It is what Paul did in Thessalonica; it is our calling as preachers. On, then, to the third word: 'demonstrating'. It is the verb *paratithymi*, which literally means 'to put alongside'. It is used, for example, of the disciples 'serving out' the food at the Lord's feeding miracles (Mark 6:41; cf. Luke 10:8; Acts 16:34). On a wholly different level, it is used when the Lord Jesus 'commits' Himself into the Father's hands (Luke 23:46), and of Paul 'committing' a command to Timothy (1 Tim. 1:18). Just as Jesus 'set out' His parables (Matt. 13:24), so Paul, in 'opening' Bible truth, 'set it out' as a coherent, persuasive case, a well-prepared and well-served meal for the mind.

The one word 'clarity' covers all three of these important verbs: clarity in addressing truth to the minds of the hearers; clarity in bringing out what the Bible says; clarity of presentation. The task is instruction; the source is the Scriptures; and the art is presentation – the truth 'served up' in a way that is palatable and orderly – 'set out' in a coherent order and shape. I can find no better description of 'exposition', no better definition of what an 'expository ministry' is all about. Whether the sermon deals with one word, one phrase, one verse, one chapter, one book or one character, the three facets of 'exposition' remain constant, and should be constantly and consciously in the preacher's mind in the study and in the pulpit. Have the hearers understood (cf., Matt. 13:51)? Has the Bible been properly and fully made plain (cf., 2 Tim. 4:17)? Has the material been set out in an orderly fashion (cf. Acts 11:4; 18:26)?

The Central Truth

Just one more thing at this point: narrowness of focus. Remember the illustration of the well-dressed window? The shopkeeper has a well-stocked store but decides what one thing he is setting out to sell, and he gives it the focal place in his window – like Jesus spoke of the scribe instructed concerning the kingdom, 'bringing out of his treasure things new and old' (Matt. 13:52). This, I believe, is the characteristic of an 'exposition': what is the central truth, the one great revelation round which this word, verse, passage, chapter, book revolves? This should be the aim of all our preparatory study, and once the central truth has been discovered, all else must be subordinated to making it plain.

Take a passage like Philippians 1:12-20. A preliminary survey shows that it falls into three parts. Verse 12 looks back over the immediate past – 'the things which happened to me'. Verses 13-18 are concerned with the present: what Paul sees as he looks around the Roman church – the two parties, one loving him, the other seeking to make his life harder – and the generality of 'the brethren' emboldened in the Lord by Paul's example. Verses 19-20 look into the future: 'this will turn out'. So far so good, but we have only skated the surface of the passage, describing *what it contains*, but not yet penetrating to *what it is about*. A closer look reveals that each section has the same focus: looking back (v. 12), Paul sees that his (uniformly difficult and testing) immediate past has been controlled in the interests of – rather, purposely designed to achieve – 'the furtherance of the gospel'. NKJV's 'actually' ('really' in NIV and 'rather, in AV and RV) points in the same direction.

Remembering 'what happened', who would have thought this? Imprisonment, defamation, false accusation, shipwreck – all seem more like a hindrance to the furtherance of the gospel. But no! Paul's backward look teaches a more positive view of the believer's experiences. Next, looking around (vv. 13-18), the outward sight of parties at loggerheads speaks of division, difference and confusion, but, again, no! Paul sees that 'whether in pretence or in truth, Christ is preached'. Everything finds a central focus in Jesus and the gospel. And the same is true as the apostle looks forward: the future will be dominated by his 'earnest expectation and hope' that 'Christ will be magnified'.

You see, then, that on the one hand the passage is full of variety, interest and instruction. Each verse could become a sermon in its own right. Yet, on the other hand, in 'expounding' the whole here, there is one overriding subject, and if preachers are to be faithful to their task then this great subject must dominate all they say, and must, hopefully, be the truth their hearers carry away: the Lord Jesus Christ sovereign over events for His own sake, the uniting factor of the Church in all outward diversity, and the great Object of our devotion.

Russian Dolls

In Philippians 1:12-20, then, the same topic keeps cropping up, and therefore it would necessarily be the central thrust of an exposition of that passage. Suppose, however, you were speaking not about this or that passage or verse in Philippians but introducing the whole letter, as an encouragement to your hearers to read it for themselves. What would such an 'overview' look like? Well, to me, Philippians is like a Russian doll – so also, incidentally, is Colossians. The outer 'skin' contains an inner 'skin', and then another, and another until we come to the central doll, the 'heart' round which all the other 'skins' are wrapped. Did Paul consciously plan it like that? I guess not, for it bears all the marks of the free-flowing thoughts of a very loving letter, but, equally, I guess that the Holy Spirit imposed His own plan on Paul's spontaneous outpouring. At any rate 1:1-2 with its references to 'saints' and 'grace' is matched by 4:21-23; Paul dwells on his relationship with his Philippians in 1:3-11 and 4:14-20; in 1:12-26 and 4:10-13, he writes of himself, his own sense of living contentedly under Christ's rule; 1:27–2:4 matches 4:1-9, the Church firm and united whether assaulted from outside by foes or from inside by division; and finally, the central 'doll', the revelation of Jesus as our example (2:5-11), our righteousness (3:1-16), and our hope (3:17-21).

I find that sort of overview a real help to my own reading of Philippians and to my ability to remember clearly what the letter contains, but I also know that it can be shared, just like that, with a Sunday-morning congregation, leaving the hearers with a focus on Jesus. You can see that with an outline like that in hand a huge multitude of sermons is waiting to 'come out', but I hope even more that you can see what a potent 'turn your eyes upon Jesus' such an overview can prove to be.

Many of the things arising from our consideration of Philippians will come up later in this book but for the moment let me say that this, I believe, is the heart and essence of 'exposition' and of 'expository preaching'. The Bible is not a launching pad but a deep freeze or a super-market. A launching pad is but a starting point from which a satellite goes into a trajectory which has no more link with the pad than that it started there! We have all heard sermons like that! The deep freeze and the supermarket are storehouses from which we bring out specific goods. Like Jesus said, the scribe under the discipleship of the kingdom brings out of his treasures things old and new (Matt. 13:51-52).

Aaron undoubtedly was a daft and useless leader, but his golden calf expresses a great truth: the gold is there in Scripture, 'unfathomable mines' indeed; it is our job to expose it to the fires of our study and delight, and to watch what 'comes out' for the enrichment of the Lord's people.

Chapter 6

Getting to know you: Examination

'Examination' is the keyword for this chapter. But before we say what it means we had better sketch the way ahead just a little bit. 'Examination' will be followed by 'analysis', 'orientation', 'harvesting', 'presentation' and 'application'. Now, even though these are all distinct exercises in preparing a sermon they are not really successive steps. Rather – if I may put it this way – they are like the rails in a six-track railway. I know such a thing is impossible, but you can see what I mean: they are aspects of sermon preparation that run in parallel, and all the time while working away at one of them we are keeping all six in mind, like a sixfold track leading to our destination.

Our God-given Circumstances
But I want to inject another preliminary word – and one which I consider deeply important. We who are called to

preach work within our own God-given circumstances, experiences and possibilities. It so happens that it was (as I see it) my good fortune, under the hand of God, to love the Bible as far back as I can remember, and to learn Greek and Hebrew from outstanding teachers at an age, in each case, when anyone can learn anything. That, then, determines the way I work. My chosen versions of the Bible for study are the Hebrew Old Testament and the Greek New Testament. This does not make me more able than others, or a better preacher. It simply explains what I mean by working 'within our own circumstances, experiences, and possibilities'. Again, some of us have been given the opportunity to collect books and commentaries, and to love to use them; and some of us have been called to 'full-time' ministry and can therefore set aside hours in study and preparation, whereas others fit preparation into the smaller budget of time their daily work allows.

We will each of us react, then, to the suggestions in this book in the light of our God-given circumstances and calling, but I am afraid in case any who work within briefer limits of time and with few or no books at their disposal should think what I write has nothing to say to them. In the years following my conversion I was privileged to hear very great preaching, both from the ministers of the church where I was a member (St Kevin's Church of Ireland Church, Dublin), and also at the then very large central Brethren Assembly at Merrion Hall – affectionately known among us as 'the Hall'. Among the latter preachers some were senior men in the Assembly itself, leading busy professional lives, some were visiting preachers who often alluded to the demands of their daily work in industry and commerce. Some of these, I surmise, never ventured in their reading much beyond the Bible – and in those days nothing but the AV was on offer. And indeed all through the years I have benefited richly from men who exercised their preaching ministry on a very limited budget of time and with nothing much to aid them but the Bibles they so lovingly held in their hands. Should you fall into this category, to you, too, my brethren, I offer – indeed commend – the preaching suggestions in this book. I believe the six-lines approach is for you also. It is a practical person's way into the preaching task. It is so easy (as I well remember!) to sit looking at a verse or passage waiting, hoping for 'something to come'. Much better to adopt a practical course: the way to work at our task is examination, analysis, orientation, harvesting, presentation and application, and this applies however short the time available, however meagre the help from other quarters. It is the way to 'work with the Word'.

The Basic Task

But 'examination' comes first and is the basic task of the expositor: to understand each word, sentence and verse in a passage, each section of a narrative or book. Much depends on the cast of an individual's mind how such an examination is conducted. Some people are so fertile in mind and imagination that things like commentaries and other people's opinions are only intrusive. When I asked John Stott, long years ago, if he used commentaries much in preparation, he said, 'Not really. I find they only confuse me.' Well, yes, there are people like that, and also there are commentaries like that! But some of us – and certainly I place myself among them – have minds like the village pumps of long ago. The pump stood on the village green, and beside it a drum or bath of water and a jug. Water had to be poured into the pump to make an airlock before the pump would operate and deliver the goods. You must discover what suits you, but I confess that I am very much in the category of the village pump! Lots of input required!

Concordances

One of the chief aids available in understanding our Bibles is a good concordance, a book listing the places a word occurs in the Bible.

The great truth lying behind concordances and the use of a concordance is that 'Bible words have Bible meanings'. A standard dictionary will tell you what a word means in English, but only a concordance can tell you how a word is used in the Bible, and within what ranges of meaning. English translations often use the same rendering for different Hebrew and Greek words, and, frequently, translate the same Hebrew and Greek words with different English equivalents. Concordances are available which group the English variations under their Hebrew and Greek originals, and it is a most illuminating study to follow a word through all its biblical occurrences. In this way we are allowing Scripture to illuminate Scripture.

For example, take the word *sophron* which NKJV, AV and RV render as 'temperate' (ESV 'self-controlled') in Titus 2:2. It won't be long before your concordance leads you to Luke 8:35 where the related verb is translated as 'in his right mind', meaning 'in full possession of his faculties', 'calm' in contrast with frenzy (v. 29) and 'self-possessed' in contrast with the total disorientation of multiple demonic possession (v. 30). This casts light, does it not, on the characteristic required in the senior men of the congregation: to possess 'poise', unflappability, thoughtfulness, a balanced approach – the opposite of 'flying off the handle', making hasty, unthought-out, or rash decisions: people of safe, sound judgment.

Here is another example from a different area of study. Hebrews 2:14 says the purpose of the death of the Lord Jesus was to 'destroy' the devil. The verb is *katargeo* which also occurs, for example, in Luke 13:7 of a barren fig tree making the ground useless. Hence, the meaning 'to render ineffective, to nullify'. Pretty illuminating regarding the position of Satan!

This approach is equally useful in the Old Testament. Ezekiel 3:20, telling of a hypothetical professedly 'righteous man' who turns to wickedness, seems to say that the Lord Himself 'lays a stumbling block before him'. This troubling picture of the Lord setting out to trip someone up is seen in a different – and true – light if we use a concordance to find out about the key word. Our concordance will lead us to the verb *kashal* and the noun *mikshol*. A much more penetrating insight into the Lord's moral dealings with us emerges. In Ezekiel 7:19 and 18:30, a person's own iniquity is the tripwire which brings him down; in Jeremiah 6:19-21 the 'stumbling block' is 'the fruit of their thoughts', the merited outcome of rejecting the Lord's law, the due and just reward apportioned by the holy Lord. In other words, the *mikshol* expresses what we might call a 'holy complex' of ideas: it is an act of divine mercy, like a barrier with a notice on it that says 'Danger Ahead'; it is a moment of decision, to accept or reject divine revelation, or it is (Isa. 8:13-15) the Lord Himself; it is a point of judgment and crucial decision – pass it and you pass the point of no return.

41

Many more examples could be given, of course, but these may possibly whet the appetite by showing the importance of not resting on what a particular translation may say at any given point, but of following through the principle that 'Bible words have Bible meanings'. Later on, when we consider word study as a form of exposition, we will find that a concordance can open up wide and versatile – and very rich – vistas of fuller understanding.

Versions

What a day we live in with so many translations of the Bible readily available! Most of us settle on one favourite version for ordinary use – in my case, at the moment, NKJV. Nowadays, before going to preach at a church it is necessary to ask what version is used, what version has been made available in the pews. I recall going to a church one Eastertime intending to preach on Acts 3:26, only to find that the Bible version in use there so mistranslated that verse that it no longer made any reference to the Resurrection! But from the point of view of study and sermon preparation I would say to those whose experience under the good hand of God has not made the Hebrew and Greek of the Bible available to them, there is safety in numbers. In popular terms (not wholly accurate), the older translations and their modern revisions (AV, RV, NASB, ESV) tend towards a 'literal' or 'word-for-word' approach to translating, while more recent translations (NIV, NRSV, GNB) favour, to one degree or another, a paraphrasing approach. We, who look for help wherever we can get it, should allow each type of translation to illuminate the other. A translation like the Revised Version (1885) – still, in my view, the best English text for Bible *study* – will, in its wooden way, lay a foundation on which to work; the more paraphrasing translations contribute specific interpretations, meanings and shades of meaning, helping us to build up a picture of the whole range of truth. In the same way, if your preference is to work from one of the recent translations, do try to have on hand one of the older versions, which will help to keep your thinking grounded as near to the original languages as you can get. When Spurgeon wrote about the then newly published Revised Version of the New Testament, he remarked, 'Strong in Greek, weak in English.' I must say that just about sums up what I would look for in an English version of the Bible for the purposes of study.

Perhaps an illustration of the way translations can feed into each other may help. In 2 Timothy 3:16 NKJV, like its 'father' the AV, reads 'all Scripture is given by inspiration of God', and that, of course, is perfectly true, but to 'inspire' is to breathe truth into someone or something. The NIV adjusts our focus with 'all Scripture is God-breathed', that is to say, the Scriptures began in the mind of God and He 'breathed them out' for our learning. Or take an example that works the other way. In Philippians 2:7, NIV offers the obviously mistaken translation (astonishingly also followed by ESV) that the Lord Jesus, coming to earth, 'made himself nothing'. Tell me, how could anyone read the Gospels and then say Jesus 'made himself nothing'? We trace the course of our mighty, wonder-working Lord, we take note of His vivid and outstanding qualities, we marvel at His moral majesty, and exclaim, 'Whatever the correct translation of Philippians 2:7, that one cannot be right!' Of course it can't! NKJV has retained the emotive 'he made himself of no reputation', a touching recollection of

Isaiah 53:2-3. But RV decides in favour of the literal that He 'emptied himself', so that we watch One who was 'in the form of God' (NKJV, RV), so to speak, pouring all his divine nature into a new situation by taking 'the form of a servant' (NKJV, RV).

Commentaries

As it was noted above, we are all different, and some have such independent and fertile minds that meanings, lessons, messages and presentations flow freely out of any given word, verse or passage, but I guess most of us need the help and stimulation provided by what others have discovered. Commentaries vary in value and in reliability. It is essential to safeguard one's independence of judgment, and to determine in advance to reject anything (from whatever source or 'authority' it may come) that seems to contradict or in any way to be to the detriment of the truth, dignity, authority and sanctity of the Bible. In fact, in my gloomier moments, I think the only safe course is to believe nothing one reads or hears until one has the opportunity to 'test all things' (1 Thess. 5:21). At any rate, there is no law against suspending judgment until the Scripture makes itself clear. And, indeed, this is a wonderful aspect of our Bibles: the more we read the whole, the easier we find it to understand the part; and the deeper we delve into the part, the more we are enabled to understand the whole. Bible readers find over the course of the years that the Bible has a way of making itself plain. Perseverance and faithful, prayerful continuance in Bible reading does bring understanding. The explanation of this is that, just as the Holy Spirit sent Philip to be on hand to explain Isaiah 53 to the Ethiopian (Acts 8), the same

Spirit is graciously alongside us to open the meaning of the Bible to us. Whether He provides us with a 'Philip' – and as I write I thank God all over again for the faithful teachers He has sent to me – or brings a helpful book our way, or Himself prompts thoughts and truths in our minds, He can be relied on to be our teacher in the Word He Himself inspired.

Nevertheless, commentaries – and now, I am told, the Internet – can be our 'Philip', and we can benefit from the gifts God has given to other people, and, generally speaking, the more the merrier! We all need all the help we can get – and even when we do not agree with what someone writes, that too is a benefit, for it both rules out one line of understanding, and also forces us to explain to ourselves why we disagree. It all brings us to a better and more precise understanding; all grist to the same mill!

Conservation
One thing is very important in sermon preparation, and that is to devise a way of conserving what we are discovering. An experienced preacher gave it as his opinion that in serious preparation we actually gather seven times more material than we are able to use in one sermon! I could not prove the 'seven times', but I do know that 'more', and, indeed, 'much more' is true. All this material needs to be preserved for future use. I grew up in the pre-computer/wordprocessor age, and therefore I naturally think in terms of loose-leaf notebooks and fountain pens! I have found a fairly small page (approximately 7 by 5) best in that individual notes, thoughts, comments and extracts from commentaries can be given their own page and be kept separate from each other, but you, clever

person that you are, can doubtless do the same thing on your computer with a prompt and easy recovery system. In any case, the important thing is to lose nothing, conserve everything. Don't rely too heavily on memory. Make your notes detailed and explicit enough to make sense in twenty years' time! I have a page of sermon notes which, at one point, simply says 'Mary Magdalene'. I am confident the reference made a significant contribution to the sermon at the time (1948), but now I can't remember for the life of me what she is doing there!

My original single loose-leaf notebook (when I was working on expositions of 2 Timothy in 1964) has grown into about 250 notebooks, a continuing resource for sermon preparation (and also a quick 'refresher course' alongside daily Bible reading). Record everything, lose nothing, whether from concordances and commentaries, from your own thinking, or from listening to other peoples' sermons. Bend everything to the task of an accurate, thought-out understanding of the Word of God.

My little notebooks come in for another practical use, and I don't know where else to mention it, even though I should really apologize for its intrusion here. When I started out as a preacher I used to write my actual sermon notes on sheets of paper the same size as my Bible, and go to the pulpit with the notes safely tucked into the appropriate place in the Bible. So far so good, except that I found it so easy for separate sheets – and on one occasion the whole lot – to get swept off the smallish note desk in our pulpit and go floating off down the church! If you use detached sheets, clip them safely into a looseleaf notebook. Don't invite a disaster!

The End Result

So what are we aiming to achieve by this 'examination'?

- If we are studying a single word, then the aim is to put on paper a statement, as detailed as possible, of the way that word is used in the Bible, and what its range of meaning is.

- If we are dealing with a verse, passages or a whole book, then, again, to set down what the verse, passage or book 'covers', what it is 'all about', along with explanations or definitions of key words, and, as best we can, of any particularly difficult phrases or sections.

In getting to this point there may well be, as yet, no sign of a sermon on the way, but the ground will have been covered. This is the first step. This is the time, obviously, to do our major work with the concordance and with whatever commentaries are available. One of the major 'one-volume' Bible commentaries can be a great help if you have not yet managed to get a few books around you. Even with the limited space available when one volume tries to cover the whole Bible, it is often surprising how the authors manage to fit in explanations of hard verses – and certainly they set out to offer a running outline of books and passages.

On, then, to the next 'track'.

Chapter 7

Rightly Dividing: Analysis

More recent translations (NIV, NASB, ESV) take a 'bland' view of 2 Tim. 2:15 as meaning 'handling correctly the word of truth', and who can complain about that? It is a standard to which we would all aspire, and, besides, it is, up to a point, accurate enough. NKJV retains the rendering found in AV and RV, 'rightly dividing the word of truth', and this strikes near the mark in that the word in question *orthotomeo* is a compound of 'straightness' and 'cutting'. It only occurs elsewhere in the Bible in the Greek translation of Proverbs 3:6 and 11:5, in both places associated with the word *hodos*/'road': to cut a straight road, like the Romans did, and like our motorways attempt! But however this one word and verse may be best translated, its meaning is plain. 'Making straight cuts' and 'driving a straight road through' is an essential of 'handling correctly' the word of truth.

Let me put it this way to you: the Bible is more than the unclassified version of *Daily Light*. *Daily Light* is a wonderfully helpful compilation bringing verses and short passages together around a selected topic for each morning and evening of the year. This is a perfectly legitimate thing to do, just as it is in many ways essential to seek in our daily reading some verse or scriptural thought that particularly 'speaks' to us that day. But the Bible is a Book composed of *books*, and, like books today, this means authorship: an author's plan set out logically and followed through systematically. Finding the plan is a basic step towards finding the message.

Psalm 100

The Psalms are a good place to practise 'finding the plan'. They are, after all, deliberately, consciously written poems, meditations on a theme or on an incident. Look, for example, at Psalm 100. Count up the six invitatory commands to worship and enjoy the Lord's presence: (in NKJV) 'Make a joyful shout (v. 1) … serve (v. 2a) … come (v. 2b) … enter (v. 4a) … be thankful (v. 4b) … bless' (v. 4c). Now notice that they are in two groups of three, each group leading to an affirmation about the Lord: 'Know that the Lord is God' (v. 3) and 'For the Lord is good'(v. 5). The first affirmation is followed by two truths about us ('he made us … we are his people', v. 3), and the second by two truths about the Lord ('his mercy … his truth', v. 5). My purpose here is not to discuss what all this means in detail. For example, a full study would require us to note that there are two ways of translating verse 3b, either 'and not we ourselves' (NKJV) or 'and we are his' (NIV), and (in my opinion, rightly) to decide to accept them both (for we may be sure the author knew his own language, was aware of the ambiguity, and decided to leave it so!). No, my purpose is to share with you the sheer excitement of finding a pattern like this, and to note with you how the awareness of the pattern at once sets us on our way to grasping what the psalm is all about.

Books and People

The same approach yields dividends in every department of Bible study and preaching.

The books in the Old Testament that we call the 'histories' are, of course, fully historical and intended to be so, but from ancient times they have been classed as 'the former prophets'. So how can 'history' be 'prophecy'? The prophets were inspired to predict the future, but there is more to 'prophecy' than prediction, or, rather, prediction was just one of the ways prophets spoke out about God and brought the Word of God to bear on their contemporary scene. For that was their primary task: to declare the truth about the Lord, recall people to Him, and set their feet on the pathway of obedience to revealed truth. Even when they reached forward into the future, it was like the ministry of John the Baptist, who cried out, 'Repent, for the kingdom of heaven is at hand' (Matt. 3:2) – 'I tell you what is coming so that you may know what to do in the present to be ready for it'. Bible history is written in the same spirit: a revelation of God, His character and His ways, as seen in the events through which He led His people. It is in this light that we take the historical books of the Old Testament into the pulpit: they speak of God.

51

Preaching a whole Book

There is special value in taking a whole book as the 'text' for a sermon. It is like providing a road map whereby travellers can see where they are going; a sermon on a whole book can set up signposts and promote personal Bible reading – especially if it is followed up with a suggested plan of reading for the following week (See Appendix). And, once again, analysis is the basis of the whole exercise. Take the books of Kings, for example. They are a sort of 'national portrait gallery' of the kingdoms of the people of God, and it is a sore temptation to get sidetracked here to share with you some of the fascinating things we find in these three full-length portraits and thirty-eight snapshots, covering five centuries. However, we must be disciplined and concentrate on the 'shape' of the books, our essential starting point in preparing a sermon on them. When we stand back from the Books of Kings they look like this:

A. The disappointed hope: Imagine David come to this! (1 Kings 1:1–2:46) All that bright promise ending in such failure! The golden boy become a toothless tiger! The richly spiritual David leaving behind such a monstrous last will and testament!

B. The flawed beginning: Solomon who had it all and lost the plot (3:1–11:43)

C. The Swinging Spotlight (1 Kings 12:1– 2 Kings 24:16): Under the inadequate – indeed, nincompoop – Rehoboam, the kingdom divided into north (Israel) and south (Judah). In the northern kingdom men tended to climb on to the throne by their own abilities and ambitions, and very few of them founded anything like a dynasty. It was the kingship of the 'strong, natural leader'. In the southern kingdom the House of David handed the crown from father to son in orderly fashion. But neither the rule of gifted leaders in the north, nor the organized succession of father to son within the Davidic Covenant in the south, could produce the king the people needed to solve their problems, the hoped-for Messiah. This is the explanation of the way the books of Kings are written, now in the southern kingdom, now in the north. It is a 'hunt for the Messiah'; will this strong, ambitious man prove to be the Lord's anointed? Will the next successor of David be the long-awaited king? The books record the hunt and its failure in both kingdoms.

B1. The inevitable end: Destruction (2 Kings 24:17–25:26) both in the north and the south.

A1. The tiny spark of hope (2 Kings 25:27-30).

Not only is it extremely satisfying to see two long books in this way, as one coherent plan, but an accurate analysis like this brings to the fore significance that might otherwise be missed. The concluding verses of 2 Kings can so easily 'slip off the tongue' as just another – even if welcome and unexpected – historical detail. Indeed, if they are taken in isolation we might easily be diverted on to a wrong road. It is natural that our imaginations be caught by the 37-year-long imprisonment of Jehoiachin. Poor lad! The 'three months' king, imprisoned at eighteen (24:8), released in his fifties! What a life! Well, the picture is moving, and the truth behind it frightening: he did evil in the sight of the Lord and paid the price. But in the light of the structure of the two books, where the freeing of Jehoiachin is seen in contrast with the bondage of the senile David, it is not the imprisonment but the release that shines out, not the dire 'due reward of his deeds' but the sovereign faithfulness of the God who does not forget, never fails to keep His promises, who is not thrown off course by the failure even of the favoured and beloved David, but rather, as that strange figure Balaam put it: 'God is not a man, that he should lie, nor a son of man that he should repent. Has he said, and will he not do it? Or has he spoken, and will he not make it good?' (Num. 23:19). The centuries of the failure of the Davidic House in the south, and of Israel's 'strong, natural leaders' in the north, do not cancel hope; the promises still stand and will be kept.

The essential 'message' of 1 and 2 Kings lies in the structure of the books, and this can so easily be shared with a congregation in one sermon – after which, almost incidentally, they will be encouraged to read the stories of Kings with new enthusiasm and understanding.

Character Studies: Preaching a Person
The Bible is full of great, colourful characters, and whether for a series of sermons or one-off occasions, character studies form one of the most interesting (including for our congregations) sources of Bible teaching. They are like extended illustrations of truth! Very often the 'message' of an individual life emerges from the shape in which the author couches the stories. Take, for example, the life of David. Simply make a list of all the stories about David in the order they come in the Bible, from his first

appearance in 1 Samuel 16 until his death in 1 Kings 2 and you will find that they form a 'trajectory': first David on the 'up and up', and then David on the slippery slope. The upward pathway begins with his secret anointing in 1 Samuel 16 and leads, through many trials, to his sudden leap to the throne in 2 Samuel 4–5. But (sadly) David the king begins to think in royal clichés – 'have army, will fight' (2 Sam. 3–4); 'am king, will send army' (2 Sam. 11) – until we find him lounging around at home in monarchical ease (11:1) while Joab takes the field, and, of course, Satan finds mischief for idle hands to do! Enter Bathsheba (2 Sam. 11), whom, possibly, David could not help seeing (v. 2), but he could help watching! From that moment he was on the downward slope with his family, his kingdom, his kingship and his person successively falling apart. See how the message is in the 'shape' of the story? Every incident has its own truth to tell and every incident could be the subject of its own sermon, but if you are preaching the whole characterization of the king, it is this sort of overall analysis that provides the revelation of truth. The message of the private failure of the public man is more than relevant to our times in which leading figures insist that what is private is strictly private and a man must be judged on how he does his job. Not so, says the story of David: the private failure, the 'thing that displeased the LORD' (2 Sam. 11:27), brought the whole fabric down – private, public, personal, domestic, individual, national.

Mary Magdalene

It is pretty amazing how many Bible books and passages have the sort of chiastic arrangement we saw in

1 and 2 Kings, or the 'trajectory' pattern we saw in David, but those of us blessed with the benign virus of Bible analysis must always be careful to let patterns emerge, not to impose alien grids on what we are studying. Most passages simply proceed from one point to another in sequence, building up to a full picture, or are linked topically rather than structurally – like the five references to Mary Magdalene. Let John 11:2 provide the 'anchor', and track your way through Luke 7:37-38; 10:38-39; John 11:32; 12:3. Did you notice that all these verses have one thing in common? Whenever Mary comes on the scene – and I am treating all five references as referring to the same Mary, which I believe to be the correct interpretation – she is 'at Jesus' feet'. Respectively, the place of beginning – gratitude for sins forgiven; of continuance – hearing His Word; of comfort in the day of trouble; and of total devotion, holding nothing back in love for the Lord. I promise you it makes a lovely sermon, and is typical of the sort of material that comes out of pondering the people on whom the Bible focuses.

Verses in Sequence
For another example of taking things as they come, but being careful to keep analysis in mind, consider the important verses of Hebrews 10:11-14. Their topic, as the context shows, is the *finished* work of Christ, and Hebrews works it out in this way:

• Finished as far as Jesus Himself is concerned (vv. 11-12a): The standing priest awaits the unending stream of clients needing 'repeat prescriptions'. But Jesus offered 'one sacrifice for sins forever' – and *sat down!*

- Finished as far as God is concerned: all requirements met (v.12b), total satisfaction in His Son and what He has done. His place at the Father's right hand speaks of acceptance, both of Himself and of His work of salvation. It endorses the Son's Calvary claim that 'It is finished.' No divine requirement has been left unsatisfied. The Son of God, the Lamb of Calvary, has been received back to the Father's right hand.

- Finished as far as Satan is concerned (v. 13): the victory has been won. The Victor is not fighting on but waiting for the great surrender.

- Finished as far as we are concerned (v. 14): Jesus has done everything to achieve our perfection, thus making our progressive experience of sanctification possible.

Hebrews 10:11-14 offers a marvellous overall 'impression' of the work of our great High Priest even when it is taken at our usual over-fast reading speed, but it is slow reading, careful analysis, that brings out the fullness and glory of what He accomplished. This involves watching out for where one topic or aspect gives way to another. For instance in verses 11-12 the contrast between 'stands' and 'sat down' is sufficient to establish the fundamental truth of the finished work of our Priest, but ask yourself this question: why does Hebrews think it important to go on to say *where* He 'sat down', namely, 'at the right hand of God'? This is not required to establish the contrast between standing and sitting, and therefore Hebrews must have introduced it in order to bring another truth into focus – as indeed it does: the moving reality of the eternal acceptance by God of what His Son, our Priest, did once for all. Jesus is (so to speak) not simply received into

PREACHING?

heaven but accorded the place of highest honour at the
Father's right hand, the proof of the Father's satisfaction
and delight in what His priestly Son has done. This is
the close attention the work of analysis requires – and
illustrates the benefit it brings.

Acts 2 revisited
Look back to pages 19-21 above where we examined
Acts 2:2-4. All too often these verses are treated to no
more than the quick reading and the casual glance. Remind
someone of Jesus' promise in Acts 1:5 that 'you shall be
baptized with the Holy Spirit' and then ask how it was
fulfilled. Promptly the answer may well come: 'In Acts 2, on
the day of Pentecost, when the Holy Spirit came, and they
spoke with tongues.' But, as we saw, in Acts 2, speaking
with tongues, the gift of intelligible communication, was
only one part of a fourfold act of the Holy Spirit on the
Day of Pentecost. It is only careful analysis that brings out
the full truth with pinpoint accuracy, and guards us from
superficial conclusions.

The Inspired Book; the Mind of the Holy Spirit
Analysis is the discovery of all the component parts
of a sentence, verse, passage, chapter or book in their
individual meaning *and in their interrelatedness*, that is to
say, how each part is related to what has preceded, leads
into what follows and throws its own light on the central
truth of the whole. In this exercise connecting words
should be noted carefully – the 'and' which adds one truth
to another, the 'for'/'because' which explains what has
preceded, and the 'therefore' which draws a conclusion.
Look at Acts 4:32-34.

- v. 32, the basic situation: a pervasive, self-subordinating fellowship, illustrated by commonality of possessions;

- v. 33, 'and', the consequential, emergent state: 'great power' in testimony to Jesus' resurrection, 'great grace' on all;

- v. 34, 'For', the explanation: the church simply would not tolerate need among its members and, at personal cost, set up a common fund, administered by the apostles to guarantee its eradication.

In this passage it is the connective words that express the 'logic' by which the Holy Spirit works – how, in His mind, one thing follows another, how one causes or gives rise to another, and, through noting the conjunctions, the verses go beyond describing what life was like in the then church to formulating a policy for creating the effective basis for evangelism, a community and fellowship worth joining.

In general the older translations (AV, RV) and some of their modern 'sons' and 'daughters' (NASB, ESV) are more careful over small words like conjunctions than some modern renderings, but the more firmly we believe the Bible to be the inspired Word of God, the more lovingly and carefully we will pause over individual words, note the conjunctions used, and trace out sequences of thought. It is words like 'and', and 'for' that express what we may call 'the logic of the Holy Spirit' – the truths He would have us hold together, the explanations He would have us ponder and the consequences that arise.

In using translations there is 'safety in numbers'. The newer translations can throw light on meanings which lie, perhaps, more obscurely in the older translations; the older translations offer a word-for-word, literal approach, providing, so to speak, a 'basic text', on which other – and freer – renderings can build, and a 'control' by which to judge the interpretations they offer. Analysis forces us to ponder detail; in the detail lies the mind of God.

Do weigh the huge benefits that can only be enjoyed by what I have called 'analysis'. It is only a fancy name for taking the details of the Bible seriously. The discussion about Acts 2:2-4 above is a case in point. Think how often the questions about when the baptism of the Spirit occurred and what it meant might be answered by a 'slapdash' reference to 'the day of Pentecost' and 'the gift of tongues', losing all reference to the rich fourfold Pentecostal work of the Holy Spirit.

'Analysis' forces us to read in a detailed way, and so to unearth the treasures of Bible knowledge.

Chapter 8

Finding the Pole Star: Orientation

This takes me back to school examinations! In a geography exam in the fourth form we could always be sure that Question One would be accompanied by an outline map of Ireland with the requirement to name all the bays and inlets round the coast, or to fill in all the rivers/lakes/mountain ranges/county towns – or whatever else came into the (to us) curious and twisted mind of the examiner. The English Literature paper always began with some slightly obscure short poem or sonnet or Shakespearean extract, with the instruction to 'read this and state what is its central idea'. I have ever remained grateful for those English teachers. Their requirement that I should find the 'central truth' has proved as significant for Bible study and expository preaching as has been the virus of Bible analysis which I caught from one of the ministers (of blessed memory) of our then church.

Here, then, is the next 'rail' on which the 'train' of expository preparation rolls forward: to discover and state the central truth in this word or passage so that it can provide the focal point round which all the other elements of teaching can cluster and be seen in their harmony – like the outline of Ireland's coast held together all the details we were required to add; and like the central truth of the poem was what gave unity to all its details. In our Bible study and sermon preparation we should learn to ask what is the 'one thing' that holds all these individual 'things' together, the one truth that they are all about.

Use 1 John 2:1-2 as an example.
It is easy to see what a cluster of treasures are assembled in 1 John 2:1-2, a sixfold revelation of the Lord Jesus Christ:

*   He is 'Advocate'. The word (as your concordance will tell you) is *parakletos*, used of the Holy Spirit in John 14:16, 26; 15:26; 16:7. Just as, by the Father's will, the Holy Spirit is positioned alongside us, the Companionate Spirit in our daily walk, so, by the same will, Jesus is positioned alongside the Father as the Guarantor of our secure place in heaven – 'I know that while in heaven he stands, No tongue can bid me thence depart'[1].

*   He is 'with the Father', demonstrating (cf., Heb. 10:12 above) the unreserved acceptance of the Saviour and of the saving work which He claimed to have finished at Calvary.

---

1   taken from the hymn, 'Before the Throne' (words by Charitie Bancroft, 1863 and music by William Bradbury, 1861).

- He is still 'Jesus', the One who, because we are 'flesh and blood himself likewise shared in the same', and is therefore the One who can be guaranteed to understand, sympathize and send appropriate aid (Heb. 2:14; 4:15-16).

- He is 'Christ', the Anointed One, i.e., qualified and equipped by God to be the Saviour of sinners, and therefore the author of a sure and guaranteed salvation.

- He is 'the righteous', and therefore able, according to the rules of the Holy God, to be our substitute, to stand in our place, pay our penalty, bear our sins, for, according to the Word of God, only the sinless can substitute for sinners: 'Your lamb must be perfect' (Exod. 12:5, literally).

- He is 'the propitiation for our sins'. I think I have only once heard the verb 'propitiate' used in ordinary conversation. It happened like this. Late on a dankish, winter afternoon in Wolverhampton where I was in my first assistantship in ministry, I met one of our menfolk with a bunch of flowers in one hand and a gift-wrapped parcel under his arm. 'What's this? What's this?' cried I, since I knew him well enough to be so familiar. 'Oh', said he, 'it's to propitiate the wife.' And there you have it in a nutshell: 'to propitiate' is to take away anger, bring back peace.

See again the value of 'slow' or 'analytic' Bible reading: pausing on each word, asking what it means, finding its particular nuance in its context. What a rich vision of Jesus and His saving work emerges here! But the key question still remains: these are all 'the things' the verses contain; what is the 'one thing' they are all about?

Years ago I was asked to judge sermons written for a prize a college was offering to its members. The set 'text' was 1 John 2:1-2. Of course, written sermons are no judge of a person's preaching ability, and, as far as that was concerned, I had to do my best to 'read between the lines' and think how this material would sound in the pulpit. As to the material itself, the decision was easier: were these scripts dealing fairly and correctly with the verses? Of the twelve candidates, eleven chose to preach about 'forgiveness', which one can obviously do on the basis of 1 John 2:1-2 – if we take them in isolation. The twelfth candidate said no, these verses are not about 'forgiveness', they are about 'assurance'. How very exact! That, for sure, set him on track to be the prizewinner! The matter can be quite simply stated even though the issues involved are themselves far from simple. According to 1 John 2:1a, the outcome of the saving work of Christ is the disappearance of sin from our lives. Consequently, should sin continue in evidence ('if anyone sins'), is not the reality of our salvation called into question? As we battle with sin and constantly lose the battle, can we credibly claim to be heirs and possessors of this great salvation?

Why, yes, we can, because (says 1 John 2:1b-2) the ground of our salvation is not in ourselves but in Jesus: 'When Satan tempts me to despair/ and tells me of the guilt within/ upward I look and see him there/ who made an end of all my sin/ … My name is graven on his hands/ my name is written on his heart/ I know that while in heaven he stands/ no tongue can bid me thence depart.'[2] That's it! That's what 1 John 2:1-2

2   'Before the Throne'.

is 'all about' – the word of assurance which today's people of God so deeply need. Of course, it is the case that truths about forgiveness and all sorts of other important and precious truths – like the reality and significance of Jesus' Ascension – can be legitimately derived from these verses, but the supreme effective power of the Word of God flows in the channel of pinpoint accuracy of understanding and presentation, taking truths in the context and connection in which the Holy Spirit has set them.

A Pastoral Decision

This is a suitable place to give an airing to an aspect of preaching to which we must return later – the presentation of the truth in a way that is tailored to the congregation to whom we are ministering. Those familiar with the more 'literal' translations of the Bible will recall how often it is recorded that Jesus 'answered and said'. His words were both a statement of the truth (He 'said') and also a response to that particular audience (He 'answered'). So it is in preaching. We have a double responsibility: first to the truth, and secondly to this particular group of people. How will they best hear this truth? How are we to shape and phrase it so that it comes home to them in a way that is palatable, that gains the most receptive hearing, and (very often, particularly this) avoids needless hurt?

In the case of 1 John 2:1-2, for example, the most obvious presentation is 'our security in an unchanging God'. This, I think, most accurately reflects what the verses were meant to do: 'I know that while in heaven he stands/ No tongue can bid me thence depart.'[3] Each of the six truths about the Lord Jesus breathes heavenly security.

---

3   'Before the Throne'.

But a great advantage that accompanies the privilege of ministering in the same congregation week by week is that the preacher becomes aware of needs, both general and individual, and, with either the whole congregation or even a single individual in mind, the emphasis might rather be 'our assurance in the face of condemning sin'. Or, again, what about a sermon on the reality and meaning of the Lord's Ascension? Either way, the passage is full of the word of comfort which is ever the task of the preacher and the need of the hearer.

Bearing in mind the needs of individuals in our care is very different from 'preaching at' somebody! I did that once, and learned a sharp lesson. On the Monday morning, on the way to post a letter, I actually met the man whose ear I had hoped to fill with truths tailored specially for him. 'Oh,' said he, 'I enjoyed your sermon last evening.' 'Well that's a bad start,' thought I. 'You shouldn't have! You weren't meant to!' 'It's a pity,' he continued, 'that them wasn't there as it was meant for!' The pulpit is no place for trying to 'get at' people. It is a place for the Word of God, sensitively and carefully fashioned and phrased for their welfare.

Another Psalm
Psalm 121 is another place where the task of analysis and the search for the central truth dovetail into a clear 'message'. Translators shy away from allowing the same English word to appear too often in close proximity. This is understandable, though, from the point of view of accurate study, regrettable. The RV, as one would expect, pursues its steady way where even NKJV 'nods'; ESV holds its nerve and follows the Hebrew (which, contrary to English, rather thrives on repetition) in its sixfold use of

the verb 'to keep'. And that is what the psalm is all about: the keeping Lord, the kept believer: the Lord who 'keeps ... keeps' (vv. 3, 4); He is 'your keeper' (v. 5); 'he will keep ... will keep ... will keep' (vv. 7, 8).

This is exactly what the unnamed watcher of the hills (v. 1) needed to hear. Was he a pilgrim envisaging the hills (potentially hiding robbers) through which he must pass to reach his goal in Zion? Was he a Jerusalemite, royal or commoner, watching anxiously, in one of Jerusalem's many crises, for the appearance of enemy banners or campfires on the hills around his city? Whatever! We do not know what danger then threatened, and, it seems to me, the Bible deliberately leaves a gap in our knowledge, in order that we may 'fill in' whatever our own current need happens to be.

We do know, however, that he faced his danger in the strength of the Lord the Creator (vv. 1, 2). This is important. In the Bible the Creator is in absolute, directive, sovereign control of the Creation. Nothing happens without His direction and permission. No threat can strike the pilgrim or the city but the Lord the Creator, knows, plans and is in charge. Furthermore, since He is the Creator, every circumstance, pleasing or hostile, happens within His world. What a message of security!

In verses 3 and 4 another aspect of protection comes to the fore. As we seek to analyse the psalm, the question must be asked why the singular 'you' suddenly becomes the collective 'Israel' in v.4. Would not 'Behold, he who keeps you' be equally apt, and indeed maybe even more pointed? So why 'Israel'? Because thought has moved on from the Lord the Creator to the Lord the Redeemer: 'Israel' is our name as His redeemed ones, those who sheltered under the blood of the Lamb (Exod. 12), the Lord's 'firstborn son' (Exod. 4:22) covered, protected and spared. Did He redeem us in order to desert us in time of danger? Or, to put the matter more pointedly in its total biblical context, did the Father give His Son for our salvation only to forget us in a time of peril? Of course not, but there is more.

In verses 5 and 6, the thought moves on yet again to the Lord our Companion, our shelter from both real (sun) and imaginary (moon) dangers as He carefully positions Himself between us and the source of harm.

Finally, the psalm makes a comprehensive statement of the Lord's keeping power, catering for all perils (v. 7a), for the whole person ('your soul', v. 7b), for all activity (v. 8a) and all time (v. 8b).

I don't need to call your attention to how deeply satisfying it is to read the Bible in this way – slowly, and with the objective of careful analysis. No, I don't need to, but I can't bear not to! It is in this way we rescue the lovely Psalm 121 from the blessed realm of a general impression to its proper function of detailed comfort and reassurance, and the full force of the sixfold 'keeping' is brought home, as central truth and detailed analysis together work their magic. Dare I pause to point out an emergent truth which, of course, must be handled with biblical sensitivity? Reading the psalm in the light of this analysis and in the context of the whole of Scripture, it is right to notice how the triple revelation of the guardian Lord as Creator, Redeemer and Companion comes to fulfilment in the New Testament revelation of the Holy Trinity.

Setting up Signposts

Preaching a whole book in one sermon encourages our hearers to read the book for themselves with new eyes – particularly if it is linked to a seven-day reading scheme circulated at the same time. See examples in the Appendix to this book.

Have you ever had someone say to you after service 'I read that verse during the week and I didn't get anything out of it like you did today'? The honest reply (which you wouldn't dream of making) is 'Of course you didn't, because you didn't spend hours sweating over it like I did!' No, indeed! You would say something encouraging, something along the lines of 'I am so grateful if you have been helped, but do keep going in your own Bible reading. The Lord will see to it that you get out of it what you need.' But the danger is there. Constantly delving ever more minutely into single verses might prove a damper to some sensitive soul, whereas setting up signposts that chart a way through a whole book can, by contrast, encourage personal Bible reading. The wood is seen, rather than this or that tree!

Amos

The book of Amos is a reasonably easy place to start. It lends itself to analysis in a particularly straightforward way. In 1:2 the LORD is envisaged as a roaring lion (a concordance will inform you that this is the lion's pouncing roar: it is almost on its prey). Now note that the roaring lion reappears in 3:8. This is called an *inclusio* – in this case a *verbal inclusio* (an identity of wording) acting as a bracket round a section. It is a frequent feature in biblical literature, and something we should be on the lookout for in Bible analysis. Let us assume, then, that Amos 1:1–3:8 forms the opening section of the book.

In the same way, 'an adversary all around the land' (3:11) finds its *inclusio* in 6:14, not now a verbal but a *thematic* match: a hostile 'nation' afflicting Israel from Hamath in the north to the Arabah valley in the south. The 'all around' of 3:11 is recapitulated in the 'north-south' of 6:14. Finally in 7:1-6 there are two visions of total destruction which 'shall not be' (vv. 3, 6), and these are balanced (*inclusio by contrast*) by visions of the glory which certainly will be, 9:11-15. So what is Amos' prophecy about?

- First (the first *inclusio*), the Lord is *active in judgment* – worldwide, over all nations (1:3–2:3) as well as over the dual kingdoms of Judah and Israel (2:4–3:8).

- Next (the second *inclusio*), Amos concurs with the world-view of the prophets, that the Lord is *sovereign in history*, controls and directs the movement of men and nations, and uses aggressors in the interests of His own moral government of the world. Note how the objective fact of enemy action in 3:11 becomes direct divine action, raising up the enemy in 6:14.

- Finally (the third *inclusio*), the Lord is *sovereign in mercy*, inflexible in purpose and unfailing in fulfilling His promises. He will never allow overwhelming dangers to destroy His people (7:1-6); on the contrary, the bright, Davidic, worldwide and eternal hope will be realised (9:11-15).

I think (and indeed know) that an overview of Amos can be presented just like that to a Sunday-morning congregation, and then the central thrust of each section can be drawn out by way of application. The 'point' in section one is the distinction between the 'crimes against humanity' of which the nations are accused – violations of conscience (1:3–2:3) – and the accusation against Judah and Israel of disobeying (2:4) and silencing (2:12) the

Word of God; the heart of the second section is the call
to repentance (4:6-11) and the call to 'meet your God'
(4:12; cf. Exod. 19:17); and the third section brings us
to the promises of God, the gathered people (9:14) and
eternal security (9:15).

I hope you begin to sense the sermon you could preach
on Amos! If so, analysis and orientation are proving their
effectiveness!

Prepare for Work

Accurate analysis of a Bible book, passage or verse is
a thing of beauty. It also has a deceptive air of simplicity.
It prompts us to say 'yes, of course!' But believe me, there
is nothing simple about arriving at that point. Campbell
Morgan – Lloyd-Jones's predecessor and at one time his
senior minister at Westminster Chapel – was a renowned
expository preacher of his day and a devotee of Bible
analysis. In fact, he produced a book entitled *The Analysed
Bible* which still repays study. I think it is in the introduction
to this book that he notes that in the course of arriving at
his analysis he will have read through the passage/book
concerned forty or fifty times. The Scriptures do not yield
up their secrets to the indolent! But what a privilege is
ours – most of all if the Lord in mercy has called us to 'full-
time' ministry of the Word.

Bear with me if I take time to guard anyone from
drawing a wrong conclusion. I can hear someone who
has read this chapter expostulating, 'It's all very well for
him. He knows Hebrew and Greek.' Well, let me tell you.
Working from the Hebrew of the Old Testament or the
Greek of the New does not make looking for the central
truth one little bit easier. It's all a matter of, first, catching

a vision: there is a central truth here to be discovered, a gem at the heart of this verse, passage or book, and then being willing to work away at finding it – the very prosaic, down-to-earth work of getting really, fully and minutely acquainted with the facts that are there.

Try the Book of Joshua
Do with 'Joshua' what we did above with the stories of David: just make a list of events in the book as they happen, and discover 'what is going on'. It makes a coherent, well-planned story. Joshua, so to say the 'hero' of the book, is introduced (1:1-9), he leads the people into Canaan (1:10–5:12). The narrative of Joshua's wars of conquest follows, in turn recording his campaigns in the centre (5:13–8:29), the south (9:13–10:43) and the north (11:1-15), after which we are given a summary of what has been achieved (11:16–12:24). Logically, the details of land distribution come next (13:1–22:34), and the book is rounded off with Joshua's farewell address, retrospect and prospect.

That list of contents is worth pursuing a little bit further. It suggests a very 'rounded' statement:

A. Joshua's introduction

   B.   Entering and Conquering

   C. Summary

   B2. Occupying and distributing

A2. Joshua's Farewell

The 'summary' lies at the heart of the book, and pretty well at the heart of the summary lies 11:23, 'Joshua took the whole land, according to all that the LORD had said to Moses'. As we will see, this assertion that it was all obedience on Joshua's part and all the fulfilment of promise on the Lord's part is as good a definition of the central truth of the book of Joshua as we will find.

So far so good, but we have yet to discover a 'message'. We have noted what happened, but not what the events and the way they are recorded mean. So have another look. An attempt at closer analysis raises an interesting question. As the above outline shows, in the 'balance' of the book, the entrance to Canaan is matched by the distribution of the land and, in a perfectly coherent way, this bracket includes Joshua's campaigns of conquest against the centre, the south and the north (5:13–11:15). The question has to be asked why this account of the campaigns is 'broken' by the 'intrusion' of the ceremony of the law at Mounts Ebal and Gerizim (8:30-35). Nothing is recorded in Old Testament history writing simply because it happened – indeed, all history writing, in the Bible or outside, is essentially and necessarily a process of selection. Therefore, 8:30-35 is not recorded at that point just because it happened then. History writing does not work that way. The same applies to the incident of the circumcision in 5:1-12. What a crazy thing to do – to immobilize your fighting men as soon as you set foot in a hostile land! And now to gather the whole people in the middle of that land with undefeated enemy forces ready to pounce from south and north!

Factors of overriding importance are plainly at work. As soon as Israel enters the promised land its members must be marked as those to whom the promise has been made – this is the significance of circumcision, the marking out of the people of the promise. And as soon as they gain access to the chosen mountains of Ebal and

Gerizim (cf., Deut. 11:29) the Word of God must be made the central feature of the promised land and the people marked by circumcision as the people of the promise must identify themselves as the people of the law and of the book in which the law is written. Their occupation of the land is a matter of grace – the grace which promised the land to them – and they must be marked out as the people of grace, those to whom the promise has been made. Also, even before the land is theirs, they must affirm what life in this land is to be: a life of obedience to a revealed and written law.

But this is also the 'bracket' within which the whole book is embraced. At the beginning Joshua is commanded that the 'Book of the Law' is not to 'depart from his mouth', but is to be his daily and nightly meditation, the subject of his obedience, and the guarantee of his success (1:7-8); and, at the end, the object of his farewell address is to reaffirm the book of the law of God as the rule and guide of his people's life, their obedience (24:24-27).

Now notice that within the narratives in the book of Joshua, in the course of his astonishingly successful career, there were only two occasions of failure. The first was the attack on Ai (7:1–8:30) where Joshua acted without a command of the Lord, rather simply doing the next logical thing as a military man, and led only by military advice (7:3). Secondly, the treaty with the Gibeonites where it says explicitly 'they did not ask counsel of the LORD' (9:14). Fascinatingly, the Hebrew here says 'they did not ask the mouth of the LORD', implying that had they done so He would have spoken.

Thus a pattern emerges: Joshua is commissioned to be a man of the book (1:7-8) and, on that basis, is promised success; he deliberately centralizes the life of the people on the book (8:30-35) and ends his ministry to them by summoning them to obedience to the book (24:24-28); he meets with the success he has been promised, except when he failed to wait for or to seek the word of the Lord.

We shall be back, presently, to that word 'emerges', but just for now, what an example the book of Joshua is of the fruitfulness of approaching the text through analysis, and watching the way in which an accurate analysis exposes the central thought. Why, we are well on our way to a sermon, are we not?

Chapter 9

Gather Ye Rosebuds: Harvesting

There comes a moment in sermon preparation when, at long last (in my case, at *very* long last!), it begins to become clear what the chosen Scripture is all about. Enough material has been fed into the poor old village pump for, finally, some slight trickle to begin to come out – and we start to put on paper the fruits of our labour. This may, in fact, turn out to be the form in which the sermon is going to be preached – I think it probable that the further one gets along the preaching road the more likely it becomes that this initial 'harvesting' merges into (the topic of our next chapter) 'presentation'. But let's not be too ambitious. We have been casting our gold into the fire; something is beginning to come out. Most likely, as in the case of poor, silly Aaron's calf, it will still need a great deal of final and detailed work with an engraving tool (Exod. 32:4) before it can be called a finished product – but it will be itself the finest gold!

For instance
An example of what I mean may help. The opening verses of Psalm 51 exemplify quite a few of the procedures which have been sketched out in the preceding chapters. 'Examination' reveals that these verses contain nine significant words. In NKJV they are translated mercy, loving kindness, tender mercies, blot out, transgressions, wash thoroughly, iniquity, cleanse and sin. Moving forward along the twin lines of 'examination' and 'analysis', we find here:

• Three words describing what we may class generally as 'sin'. A bit (!) of concordance work reveals that the word translated 'sin', while it is mostly used in its moral sense, has the secular meaning of 'missing a target' (Judg. 20:16). This is a real clue to its meaning in biblical ethics: 'sin' is the specific failure – in whatever way: thought, word, deed, relationships, imagination, something done, something not done, whatever – whereby we miss God's target, veering to this side or that, undershooting, overshooting, as Paul says 'falling short of the glory of God' (Rom. 3:23). 'Sin' is the particular matter we confess: 'I am sorry for *that*'. The noun translated 'iniquity' comes from a verb meaning 'to bend, twist' (cf., Lam. 3:9; Isa. 24:1). In its ethical use it 'internalizes' our problem of 'sin', indicating that 'sin' arises from a basic flaw, a warp in human nature, which (Ps. 51:5) was there at the very moments of conception and birth, and throughout our lives lies at the root of every individual 'missing the target'. Our concordance reveals that the third word, 'transgressions', describes the revolt of a subordinate against an overlord (cf., 2 Kings 3:7; 8:20). It would therefore be more accurately and revealingly translated 'wilful rebellion' – our wrongdoing is more than a fact or event ('sin'); it cannot be blandly excused as the inevitable product of our fallen nature ('iniquity'); it is chosen, conscious, deliberate, knowing rebellion!

• Three words describing what the sinner seeks from God: NKJV 'mercy' is more properly 'grace', signifying, in the Old Testament, exactly what it means in the New: the freely given, unmerited, undeserved, unearned goodness, forbearance and forgiveness of God. The concordance will start you off at Genesis 6:8, where Noah, though a party to the wickedness of humankind (v. 5), a grief to the LORD (v. 6), and subject to His wrath (v. 7), nevertheless 'found grace'. 'Loving kindness' (*chesed*) and 'tender mercy' (*rachamim*) tell us that there are two ways of thinking of God's love, as, indeed, of ours. There is 'tender mercy', i.e., 'being in love', the love of the beating heart. The word is related to that for the 'womb', and describes surging, passionate love, like the maternal love in 1 Kings 3:26, emotional, overwhelming love. There is also, however, 'loving kindness', love as an expression of the will. This is the commitment of love affirmed, for example, in the marriage service; the love which pledges itself to remain unchanged 'till death us do part'; the love which decides, saying 'I will'.

- Three words for what is asked from God: 'blot out, wash thoroughly, cleanse'. To 'blot out' (in 2 Kings 21:13 of wiping a plate clean) points to sin as leaving a mark that God can see, and that He can wipe away. To 'wash' is a launderer's verb and here teaches that there is, so to speak, a moral detergent known to God that pursues and removes every last trace of sin right down into the fibres (Heb. 9:14). 'Cleanse', you will find, is characteristically a Levitical verb, expressing the idea of sin as a barrier to relationships, and this, too, God can deal with.

A Sermon Emerging

All this is a good testing ground and illustration of pretty well everything in the preceding chapters. We have *examined* the passage and noted the nine words. With the help of a concordance we have *explained* the words, gathered their meaning – and, in some cases, the range of meaning of each word. In the course of this we will, of course, have gathered so much more information about the meaning of the words than can be used in a single sermon, and stored it away for the future.

It is also plain that this material can be 'beamed' in different directions to meet different needs: will it be a sermon, for example, on the sickness and cure of fallen human nature, or on the wonder of a saving God? Or will we take note of the fact that verse 3, beginning with the 'explanatory' 'for', invites us to preach on the effectiveness of simple repentance? Certainly, it seems, once we have done the spadework, noted the bearing of the three sets of key words, and decided the target to aim at, this sermon is pretty well going to preach itself.

Psalm 119

Briefly consider another example of a sermon 'emerging' from the basic work of examination, this time in Psalm 119. This exposition, of course, could probably be drawn from any section of this wonderful psalm for, as you know, almost every verse contains some sort of reference to God's word of truth, and the vocabulary remains the same throughout. But my most recent effort 'emerged' from verses 9-16, which were prescribed to me as the chosen Scripture reading for a particular 'Bible Sunday' service. The great leading words here are (as offered in NKJV)

- verses 9, 11: 'your word'. Your excellent friends Mr Young and Mr Strong with their concordances will inform you that two different Hebrew words are used here, nouns, respectively from the Hebrew verbs 'to speak' and 'to say'. It would be impossible to draw any distinction between them. Both affirm that 'God has spoken'; He is 'the God who Speaks', or, in a more technical expression, His self-revelation is 'propositional', given in verbal, grammatical, idiomatic, intelligible form – not just significant acts which leave their interpretation open for us to make as best we can, but words, sentences, propositions addressed to the mind and understanding. Note, for example, how Exodus 3–4 come before Exodus 5–12. The LORD first tells Moses what He purposes to do, and then does it. The word of truth comes first, the confirmatory deeds follow. The 'God who speaks' comes before the 'God who acts'.

- verse 10: 'commandments'. God's word of truth spoken as an imperative, the word designed for our obedience, God's word as our obligation.

PREACHING?

- verse 12: 'Statutes' comes from the verb 'to engrave' (on a rock or tablet, Ezek. 4:1) or to 'inscribe' in a book (Isa. 30:8). It points to the permanence, the unchangeability and the fixity of God's Word.

- verse 13: 'Judgments' is a hugely important word in the Old Testament. Guard against any tendency to link it in any automatic way with condemnatory judgment or (as some recent translations tend to do) with 'justice', presumably signifying equitable social government. Its parent verb means to make an authoritative decision. The verb belongs to the judge on the bench, the king on the throne and (especially) to God in heaven. When He makes authoritative decisions they become part of the 'truth unchanged, unchanging' He reveals to His people – whether commands or principles. So, for example, Deuteronomy 5:1 speaks of the revelation God granted through Moses as 'judgments'. Try this meaning out in Isaiah 42:1, 3, 4 where even NKJV offers 'justice', but where the context requires the meaning that the Servant of the Lord brings to the Gentile world the truth about God, the revealed truth they previously lacked. Here in Psalm 119:13 the meaning is plain, indeed basic: the Lord has *spoken authoritatively*. 'The judgments of your mouth' are the matters He has settled by His divine authoritative decision, and then has spoken to His people His revealed truth.

- verse 14: 'Testimonies' is most simply understood as the Lord offering a testimony about Himself, 'making his testimony', letting us know who and what He is.

- verses 14, 15 use two different words translated 'way' and 'ways'. The former is usually rendered 'road' and the latter 'path'. Both are metaphorical of character-istic behaviour or typical lifestyle, just as we say of someone, 'it's his way'.

* verse 15: 'Precepts'. The versatility of this word makes it, in one sense, hard to pin down. The 'parent' verb (*paqad*) is used of the Lord 'visiting' His people mostly in kindness and care (Gen. 21:1), but also in serious examination and sentencing (Amos 3:2). It is used also of 'numbering' (Exod. 30:12). Possibly the basic sense is to give detailed attention to. Through His Word the Lord searches His people's hearts, cares for them, rebukes, but knows them all individually 'by number', as though He Himself had taken a census of them. But, in relation to us, 'precepts' points to our attention to the detail of His Word, its application in detail to our lives.

What a glorious passage to be offered for 'Bible Sunday'! Having isolated and defined the key words, can you see sermons emerging? Yes indeed, with at least two possi-bilities. If we are looking for a sermon on the Bible itself, very powerful truths present themselves – the Bible's *uniqueness* as the very 'word' of God, from 'his mouth'; its *speciality* as the book in which the Lord 'testifies' of Himself; its *authority*, directing our lives by its revealed 'statutes' and 'judgments', 'precepts' and 'commands'; its *transforming power* (Ps. 119:9, 11), cleansing and re-straining from sin.

Alternatively, there is helpful instruction here on how we should use the Bible in daily reading – expecting the Lord to teach (v. 12), opening our minds in unhurried meditation (v. 15), storing the word in memory (v. 11), delighting emotionally in Bible truth (vv. 11, 14, 16), pondering and applying its details (v. 15).

In a word, once 'examination' has done its work, there is truth to be harvested, even the possibility of different harvests from the same passage.

Just a Word

Far be it from me to labour the point, but you do see, don't you, how the procedures of examination, orientation and harvesting, as we have called them, allow sermons to 'emerge' out of texts and passages? This, surely, is the very essence of 'exposition'.

In the light of the illustrations above from Psalms 51 and 119, I ought to say something here about word study as a particular form of expository ministry. Since this sort of exposition involves looking up verses, and encouraging hearers to do the same, it is particularly suited to a small group or a midweek Bible study, but certainly not only so. Churches now tend to provide Bibles in the pews, and this makes it easier for the preacher to call out page numbers, and so facilitate audience participation. I find myself a little bit ambivalent, actually, about this sort of general provision of Bibles, because the older custom, in which I grew up, and which I still follow, was to bring one's own Bible to church, and that is still my preference. I can't imagine going anywhere without my own Bible! But the advantage of providing one version for the whole church is that it makes more readily possible the sort of exposition that involves the hearers in hunting out verses and looking up passages, and following page numbers. Congregations ought, in any case, to be encouraged to do this: it is our obedience to the scriptural injunction to 'test all things' (1 Thess. 5:21) – or, as I say in my rasher moments, 'Never trust a preacher! Make sure what is being said is in the Bible!' At any rate, word study is not only a serious form of exposition, but a very instructive and potentially fascinating one.

'Faithful'

Take, for example, the word 'faithful' (*pistos*). When it is applied to individuals its meaning hovers between 'believing' and 'trustworthy', and it is not always easy (maybe not even necessary) to settle on one rather than the other. But when God is described as *pistos* a very interesting word study is launched. The concordance allows a whole group of verses to gather, say, round the expression 'God is faithful', as found in 1 Corinthians 1:9 as a starting point. In 1 John 1:9 He is 'faithful to forgive' (cf., Heb. 2:17); in 2 Thessalonians 3:3, faithful to 'guard from the evil one' (cf., 1 Cor. 10:13; 2 Tim. 2:13); faithful to His promises (2 Cor. 1:18-20 cf., Heb. 10:23); and faithful in bringing us home to glory (1 Thess. 5:23-24). And there are others – too many to be considered in one sermon. Do you know the proverb that 'though the tongue never tires, the ear does'? We need to heed it in our preaching, even if we don't always manage to obey it!

Galatians 4:4

I call this sort of word study 'concordance preaching' – and, between ourselves, if you are ever 'caught on the hop' for a sermon, it is a very efficient way to gather scriptural material at speed! The same method can be used on a topical basis. There are three components in the great verse, Galatians 4:4 – God, the woman and the birth. The truth of the sending God can be developed, for example, with the help of 1 John 4:9-14; 'the woman' leads us back to Luke 1:31-38; and the birth – or 'the becoming' (for you will discover that this is the verb that is used) – 'become from a woman, become under the law' – can be linked with such verses as John 1:14, 2 Corinthians 5:21, Galatians 3:13.

Proper Titles

The 'proper title' for 'concordance preaching' is 'exposition by association' – which has a much more important ring to it as well as being more accurate. Our essential aim is always 'exposition' – bringing out, or allowing to emerge, what is already there. Wherever or whatever, this aim must dominate. You have the privilege of bringing a Scripture reading and what the Scots might call 'a wee wordie' to open a committee meeting, and naturally you will choose a passage appropriate to that committee and that agenda, so be very careful. Is the topic genuinely there waiting to emerge? We must not force Scripture into our mould, but rather submit to Scripture moulding us, our thoughts, discussions and decisions. Are we visiting in a home, sitting at the fireside, ministering at a hospital bed? Wherever we are, we are there as ministers of the Word of God with the aim of bowing under the truth the Word declares. Like a doctor who pays a house call with his 'bag of tricks' in his hand, so we go into people's houses Bible in hand. That is what we have come to bring; that is what we are for. How well I remember my early days in ministry, before I learned the importance of 'the Bible in the hand', desperately trying to 'bring the conversation round' to the point where it would be natural to fetch my pocket Bible out of my pocket! Bible in hand, the situation is reversed: those we visit are waiting for the moment when the book will be opened! But the material point is – that is what we are for: to 'open the Book'. A lady said to me, speaking of the minister at her church who had just moved on: 'I don't know what we will do without Mr. X. He used to explain the Bible to us.' An epitaph to be coveted!

Exposition by Topic or in Sequence

Recall the material above on Psalm 119. That should be called 'exposition by topic', where, after we have done all the basic preparatory work of examination and analysis, the harvested truth begins to present itself as a series of topics drawn from here and there in the gathered material. Probably, however, most sermons fall into the category of 'exposition in sequence' – taking the verse or passage point by point in the order in which it appears (as with Gal. 4:4). Shame on me, I have never expounded my way through Galatians nor preached from Galatians 5:16-25, but I see from my notebook that my own study of it has reached the point where an expository sermon could well begin to emerge. In my NKJV the paragraph is entitled 'Walking in the Spirit'. Very well, what is 'walking in the Spirit'? It is first (vv. 16-18) a constant tension and battle. Like the Lord Jesus in Luke 4:1, we too will find that the personal indwelling of the Holy Spirit is the start of an unending battle. Paul specifies the irreconcilable opposition of flesh and Spirit. In this battle, according to verses 19-23, contrasting possibilities lie before us: the works of the flesh or the fruit of the Spirit. The battle constantly forces us to take sides, make choices, flee the one and follow the other. Finally, verses 24-25 offer us a diagnosis of who and what we are if we belong to Jesus (v. 24), and give us a directive for our lives (v. 25): we have a transformed status (v. 24), and a summons to live by new rules (the meaning of *stoicheo*, NKJV 'walk'), i.e., those of the Holy Spirit.

It remains, of course, to work all this up into an expository sermon, but, on the face of it, it is likely that one would take the passage section by section in sequence, because it consists of such clear points of truth one after another. The separate issue of 'orientation', of course, may take over, depending on the occasion. If, for example, it was a beginners' group needing instruction about the place and work of the Holy Spirit in the believer's life, the presentation would probably be best if taken point by point in sequence. If, on the other hand, it was a group who had received erroneous teaching about the Holy Spirit and were therefore entertaining wrong expectations, there would be a need to stress the element of conflict, battle and choice. The material would be the same, but the sermon would possibly start with verses 19-23 as being the place where wrong and perilous expectations could be immediately corrected.

I would have to say that sermon preparation sounds all too easy when it is put like this. If my experience is anything to go by, nothing about preaching is easy! Indeed ,I would have to warn you that when the nuggets of truth which will eventually become your sermon begin to 'emerge', the hardest work of all is about to begin! But that is the subject of our next chapter.

Chapter 10

The Window and the Cake: Presentation

The *reason* for preaching is the will of God: He has commanded it; the *content* of preaching is the Bible, God's revealed truth; the *objective* of preaching is application, to bring the Word of God to bear on the hearers; but the *art* of preaching is presentation.

Long pages ago I suggested that preaching is like dressing a window or baking a cake. I am not a great hand with illustrations but those two make sense to me. We would never put the ingredients of the cake on the table for our guests, but I have heard sermons like that! It is as though the preacher, having noticed that the verse or passage falls into three or four parts (the ingredients) and having found some sort of heading (maybe even an alliteration!) for each part, considers that the sermon is prepared, and sallies into the pulpit. But headings don't make a sermon, no more than ingredients make a cake! What about the bits under each heading? So our preacher gets to his second section and we hear him say, 'Oh, I should have mentioned to you that …'. In other words, he has not prepared his presentation. Everything becomes increasingly slapdash, and our old enemy, 'muddle', wins.

In a well-dressed window every item is in its proper, chosen place; in a well-baked cake every ingredient has been added into the mixture in the proper order and proportion. 'Muddle' is the characteristic mark of the ill-dressed window, the careless baker and the bad sermon. The antidote to muddle is considered, planned, well-thought-out presentation. Yes indeed, the *art* of preaching is presentation.

Headings
Though a sermon is much more than its headings, the headings are exceedingly important. One aspect of our preparation is analysing the book, passage, verse or word into its constituent parts, and then, as we ponder it, stating clearly to ourselves what each part is about and how it relates to the main theme. Frequently these initial summary statements of the individual sections become finally the headings we share with our hearers.

Take, for example, Matthew 9:1-8, the incident of the paralytic carried to Jesus. The story is told in three 'movements':

- the paralysed man and Jesus (vv. 1-2): his condition, how he was brought, what Jesus said to him;

- the scribes and Jesus (vv. 3-7): His perception of their thoughts; His revelation of Himself in power to forgive sins;

- the people and Jesus (v. 8): how they responded in praise to God; what they testified to having seen.

I suppose the sermon could be preached like that, but, generally speaking, headings of this sort are, to say the least, less than the best. They describe what is happening; they say nothing regarding the meaning of what is happening. If a hearer should recall that the story is, in turn, about the sick man, the scribes and the people, he is actually remembering nothing of value. 'Descriptive' headings say what is happening in a verse/passage, whereas we should aim at 'didactic' headings, succinct statements of meaning and truth. So look at the story again. The descriptive headings were correct in making the Lord Jesus Christ the central thought, the linking theme of the incident. That is true, but, penetrate further in: what is He doing? He is forgiving sin; He is insisting on His power to forgive sin, and this is the power the people should have marvelled at if only they had eyes to see it. Now, how will you present that, the 'real' central truth?

My notes tell me I have preached this sermon fourteen times (so far). Usually it has been a sermon on 'The Joy of Forgiveness' ('Son, be of good cheer! Your sins are forgiven.'). A couple of times – preaching in churches which made a point of marking the first day of Lent, 'Ash' Wednesday and all that – the title was 'Have a Happy Ash Wednesday!' Once it was given an airing as 'The Surprising Jesus', and that, in fact, has usually been the opening or introduction: a man is brought who would surely say his outstanding need was healing. His four bearers would surely have said the same, but Jesus urges a man, still paralysed, to be glad that his sins are forgiven!

Different headings then 'emerged' as a way to tell the story and bring out its teaching: nothing more *joyful* than the forgiveness of sins; nothing more *divine*; nothing more *assured*; nothing more *individual*.

Well that's how I did it, but remember what a personal thing preaching is. You do it your way, but do try to make your headings brief statements of truth, part of your teaching exercise.

Varying the Diet

This is as good a place as any to raise a small warning against sameness. To me sausages, mashed potato and a rich gravy constitute one of the world's great tastes. I am a person of simple pleasures! But even I would find an unvaried daily menu of sausages, mashed potato and gravy somewhat on the tedious side! A careful cook varies the diet and varies the presentation, tempting the appetite, so as to encourage hearty eating.

Take alliteration, for example. It is an effective way to try to make our headings memorable – and this is a desirable objective and a covetable achievement when it works. But how tiresome alliteration is if every sermon is presented that way! We as a family sat under such a ministry at one period. The material itself could not have been more biblical, the diet of truth more wholesome, or indeed the preacher more dear to us, but in the car on the way home we used to share further points we had worked out for ourselves once we had 'twigged' what the alliterative scheme for the day was going to be! A sad confession – using the Scriptures as if they were a word game – and I guess we were not alone in our guilt. Alliteration has other hazards if it becomes an obsession.

It can so easily become forced and artificial – words being used not because they are exact and apt but because they begin with the appropriate letter, and an alliterative scheme can give a spurious unity to three or four entirely disparate thoughts which have little or nothing to do with each other – and maybe no more than an alliterative link with the passage itself. Alliteration is often a good servant, always a bad master. It is far better to present a plain (even if seemingly less clever) statement of a truth than to force it into an artificially imposed mould.

Aids to memory

Yet alliteration can be a memorable and 'snappy' way of impressing truth on our hearers – and this is a major point to bear in mind when we are composing headings. They are an *aide-memoire*, first and foremost to the congregation, but also (more of this later) to the preacher.

Nowadays I do some of my preaching in, if you will understand me, other people's churches. This is far from ideal, because, in my opinion, there is nothing to compare with ministering Sunday by Sunday to the same (and, God willing, growing) congregation, where knowledge and love go hand in hand to make the preaching sensitive, relevant and acceptable. It is a different sort of privilege to be incorporated into someone else's series of sermons. Thus I found myself recently obliged to preach on Colossians 1:24–2:5. An allocation of twenty-five minutes for such close-packed material as Colossians is a tall order and requires what nowadays is called 'cutting to the chase'. 'Examination' and 'analysis' brought two pretty obvious things to mind: first, that in the eleven verses one word occurred three times – the word 'mystery'

(vv. 26, 27, 2); secondly, that while Jesus dominated the whole passage, the major truths about Him which Paul was concerned to share at this point came in 1:27–2:2 – His indwelling in the believer and the 'hope' it brings (v. 27), and Christ as the repository of 'all the treasures of wisdom and knowledge' (v. 3). It seemed to me that this was about all that could reasonably be covered in the time, but that, also, it made up the 'central' truth of the passage. Consequently there 'emerged' a three-point sermon: what does 'mystery' mean? What is our position as indwelt by Christ? And what place should He occupy in our lives? Hence: a Secret (the 'mystery' is not a puzzle to be solved but a secret truth that has been revealed); a Security (the indwelling Christ brings 'hope' which, in the Bible, means certainty of outcome, uncertainty of timing); and a Sufficiency (if the fullness dwells in Him, then our task is to 'turn our eyes' constantly 'on Jesus. Look full in his wonderful face.'). Alliteration has its place.

Verging towards alliteration, but much, much more helpful, are headings which have a matching symmetry, so that each is a help towards remembering another. I find that this features a lot in my notes. Here is an example from the Gospels. For a person who cannot abide even the thought of travelling by sea, I find myself strangely drawn to the seafaring incidents in the life of our Lord. Mark 6:45-52 has proved a happy hunting ground (and, please God, a helpful one) for sermons. Take verse 48, for example. Analysis shows that this verse rests on three facts about the Lord Jesus Christ: (1) He saw them straining; (2) He came to them; (3) Walking on the sea. Let the truth emerge: (1) Jesus is aware of our difficulties; (2) He comes to us of His own volition; (3) He is not limited by the things that limit and defeat us. Now turn those three truths into headings suitable for preaching: (1) He is not forgetful, watching from the hills, seeing their distress; (2) He is not defeated, for while they cannot make headway, He walks easily to reach them; (3) He is not limited: the sea bars their progress; He walks on it. Alternatively, (1) the love of Jesus; (2) the power of Jesus; (3) the greatness of Jesus. Now whatever you may think of this as a sermon, do see how it exemplifies 'matching' headings which at least make a contribution towards memorability. A further decision remains in what order to present these points, but that depends on our knowledge of the situation to which we are called to preach.

To sum up (so far): avoid headings that merely describe what is happening in a passage or story. Far be it from me to say anything derogatory about Campbell Morgan, who stood so firmly for the Word of God when such a stand invited scorn, but no one could produce *The Analysed Bible* without some bits being less satisfactory than others. So, when at Malachi 2:1 (if my memory serves) he tells us that 'at this point the prophet turns from the people to the priests', he has, in fact, told us nothing; he has merely said what is happening. Make your headings *do something*. As we have seen above, one thing they can do is affirm truth.

Another thing they can do is apply the truth to the hearer: applicatory headings. I find I have not used this approach a lot – and it does not surprise me, because I am not comfortable with the 'you' approach to preaching. We are not like doctors diagnosing and prescribing for someone else's complaint – in which case 'you' is appropriate and necessary. We who preach are fellow-sufferers from the same disease! 'We' is the generally appropriate form of address. Between ourselves, I have heard some preachers who, to tell you the truth, I would as soon go twelve rounds with Muhammad Ali as be battered around the ears again by them. Our calling is not to bruise but to heal the Lord's people! So, in one sermon which adopted applicatory headings, I recall that I was careful to say at each point, 'This, then, is what the Bible commands us,' and, when moving to another point in the sermon, 'What else does this story command us?' It is a sermon on the story of Philip and the Ethiopian eunuch and focuses on Acts 8:30-31. I think it was prepared in order to fit in with a series at the church to which I was invited, but if it gets another airing it will be for Bible Sunday. It worked out like this: 'Be sensible' (recognize the importance of the Bible – i.e., like the eunuch who bought himself a present of Isaiah to take home); 'Be realistic' (accept that there is much in the Bible we won't easily understand); 'Be positive' (keep on reading nevertheless. If the eunuch had persevered beyond Isaiah 53:7 he would soon have reached the highly relevant Isaiah 56:4-5. There's always something we can understand and which speaks directly to us); 'Be humble' (accept help when it is offered – other people, commentaries, sermons); 'Be obedient' (Bible reading leads to a life submissive to what the Bible commands, Acts 8:36); 'Be confident' (The Holy Spirit will send help to you like He sent Philip to the Ethiopian).

Enough, then, about headings. Just think about what you are doing; make your headings work so as to affirm, assert and apply the truth. And, of course – again – be careful to avoid sameness. Listening to a very well-known (and extremely effective) preacher (now in glory) I noticed that there were always three points and, when he came to the third, he would repeat the first two, say an emphatic 'and', and then announce his third heading. Did anyone else notice this and inwardly groan 'Not again'? Be sure someone is noticing your characteristics and idiosyncrasies, and finding them less than enthusing! So, for example, don't always preach a 'three-pointer'; take them by surprise by only having two points, or one! Don't always start by announcing your heading, keep it to act as a concise summary at the end of its section. The tongue never tires, but the ear does!

Manuscripts, Notes and Pointers

At no point is preaching more individualistic than what preachers decide to take into the pulpit with them. I remember noticing that Dr Martyn Lloyd-Jones took nothing – not even his own Bible. When I asked him about this, he simply said he was brought up in the tradition where preachers could expect to find a pulpit Bible awaiting them, and were expected to use it. He did not enlarge on the absence of notes and helps to memory. We must each learn to do our own thing – whatever leaves us with liberty in our preaching, and makes the congregation feel they are being addressed without obstruction. Not, actually, that congregations mind their preachers having and using manuscripts, notes and memoranda. One person said she was somewhat assured by the sight of a notebook because it gave a bit of hope that the sermon had been prepared! They say that Jonathan Edwards, who was used by God to promote a revival, preached with a candle held in one hand and his written manuscript held up close to his weak eyes. We don't need to get 'hung up' about such matters. Nevertheless, congregations seem to like to be addressed rather than 'read to', and, from the preachers' point of view, some think they get on best with everything written out in full, others prefer notes, pointers and aids to memory, and some rely wholly on memory.

The one thing not to rely on is the inspiration of the moment. Very often it turns out on reflection not to have been an 'inspiration' at all! And sometimes at the vital moment it is simply not there, and the preacher, having 'dried up', is left floundering – a sad, dispiriting sight, and a perfectly dreadful experience. So, experiment and discover. My first senior minister was a full-manuscript man. It kept him, he said, from becoming 'diffuse', but, as I have told you, I noticed, on the two occasions when he mounted the pulpit only to find he had left his MS in the study, that, his preaching from memory was a much more fresh and exhilarating experience. In my early days, I followed his advice and example, and tried preaching from a full manuscript, until one Sunday evening, in the hymn before the sermon, I realized I could not go on with what was proving to be a bondage, so, off I sallied leaving the MS behind. After that, I have always preached from notes with headings and subheadings, and bits written out in full. As I get older and can't so readily assume that my memory is working as once it did, I find it necessary to have rather fuller notes than used to be the case.

Of course, what we do in preparation is another matter, and here many who preach from notes or from memory find it helpful, even necessary, to have written the sermon out in full. One great advantage of this is that every item of every section of the sermon has been covered. Preparation has gone beyond showcase headings. Preachers know exactly what is to be said under each heading. This is essential for true preaching. Beware of the siren voice which says 'I know what I am going to say under that heading'. This is only another form of hoping for the best, and is no way to treat the ministry of God's Word. Hence –

- prepare meticulously and in detail. Cover every section of your sermon equally.

- take into the pulpit with you whatever leaves you free to handle the material fluently, and to address your hearers in a 'face-to-face' manner.

- of course, hold your mind open to what the Holy Spirit may prompt by way of addition, subtraction or alteration, but be sure that as a general rule God will be glorified by what you have laboured over and have 'given your best shot' more than by spur-of-the-moment insertions.

Backroom and Showcase

This chapter has gone on too long. Apologies! But it is important! As preachers, the pulpit is our showcase. Too many sermons are not worth listening to because they are all showcase but without diligently prepared, pondered content; equally, too many sermons are marred because thoughtful, attractive presentation has not been given sufficient attention. The results of studious diligence are brought to the pulpit but not in an easy, digestible form; plenty of evidence of the pains that have been taken, but lacking the presentational skill the hearers need. Who was it who said 'we are called to give people to drink of the well of the water of life, but we are not called to make them drink from the bucket or chew the rope'?

Chapter 11

So what? Application

What we need in our pulpits is didactic and applicatory exposition. I know that that sounds dreadfully threatening. It is far from the language of the supermarket, or the laundrette. But: think about it, it is true!

- 'Exposition': drawing out from the Word of God what the Holy Spirit has deposited there without addition, subtraction or modification. In Acts 20 Paul uses a telling word twice over: the verb *hupostello* which means 'to hold back' or 'conceal' – 'through fear', says a lexicon of classical Greek, 'to cloak one's true thoughts', 'to prevaricate'; and one lexicon says, 'to adjust one's sails to the prevailing wind'. An excellent example of the verb is to be found in Galatians 2:12, where Peter adjusted his behaviour to suit newcomers to Antioch. Peter 'trimmed his sails' out of fear of the recently arrived visitors from Jerusalem. Not me, said Paul! Acts 20:20, 'I kept back nothing that was helpful'; verse 27, 'I have not shunned to declare the whole counsel of God'. Not for him to trim his sails to the prevailing winds, to adjust his message in the light of current trends, to add or subtract so as to suit popular demand! Hebrews 10:39 uses the derivative noun (*hupostole*): we are not 'people of adjustment', people to draw back/to trim our sails. Oh, how well that should apply to us preachers! The Word of God, pure, direct, undiluted, nothing added, nothing subtracted, nothing adjusted!

We will, of course, be on our guard against putting the truth into needlessly hurtful words – this is one great advantage of knowing the people to whom we speak – but we will not adulterate the truth itself. Note how Paul speaks of his 'many tears' in Acts 20:19 (cf. 2 Cor. 2:4; Phil. 3:18). Even if not with weeping in the pulpit, there are truths we dare not speak unless we are weeping in heart. The Lord Jesus had many things to say but kept silence because at that time they did not have the strength to bear them; they would learn them at the right time (John 16:12, 13). So also we must show ourselves sensitive to what our hearers can bear at that moment. Preaching should lift people's burdens, not add to them. Nevertheless, the truth itself is non-negotiable.

- 'Didactic': the teaching content of the Word of God made plain, the Scriptures not treated as a word game either by the preacher or the hearers, but as vital truth to be grasped with clarity in the mind. Remember Jesus' question in Matthew 13:51: 'Have you understood?' It is the test we must apply to our preaching.

- 'Applicatory': the Word of God brought home to the hearers as truth to be believed, a way of life to be followed, a rule to be obeyed, a promise to be embraced, a sin to be avoided, an example to be followed and a blessing to be enjoyed.

Our aim should be to hold these three together, to achieve them in one move, to draw out the truth of the Word of God with such accuracy and clarity that, without further elaboration, it is plain to our hearers both what the chosen Scripture *means* and *what we must do about it.* This does not preclude using summaries: 'Let us sum up what we have learned' or 'Let us ask how we should respond', but all such applications should be against the background of crystal clarity of exposition, so that such questions come as bonuses! We should aim so to state the truth that it actually needs no further application, even if helpfulness dictates that further application be offered.

Here is a statistic for you: Of about ninety-seven verbs used in the New Testament for communicating God's truth – preaching in the broadest sense of the word – at least fifty-six are declarative – verbs like *kyrusso*, to 'herald, proclaim' or *didasko*, 'to teach', even *laleo*, 'to speak, chat'. We should take into account this emphasis before we consider verbs like *parakaleo* 'to appeal, encourage' (Acts 11:23), *deomai*, 'to plead, beseech' (2 Cor. 5:20), *peitho*, 'to persuade, seek to convince' (Acts 13:43), *noutheteo*, 'to counsel' (1 Cor. 4:14). Our primary task is to make the truth plain.

The Beginning

May the Lord deliver us from a joke at the beginning of every sermon! It is understandable – and indeed a correct desire – to catch people's attention from the word 'go', and a suitable joke, or a witty form of expression is not necessarily out of place. Indeed, if people are not relaxed enough – and sufficiently at ease in their church and with their preacher – to enjoy a laugh, it is doubtful if they are really ready to open their ears to listen, learn and be blessed! 'No laughs, no blessing' would, perhaps, be a bit extreme, but it verges on the truth, and certainly if people feel it improper to laugh in church it is doubtful if they have learned to enjoy the Scriptures. The stiffness, the wooden solemnity, the oppressive seriousness one meets with in some churches militates against true hearing and joy in the Lord and His truth. It is one thing 'to play it for laughs'; it is another thing never to experience and share joy – even a giggle or hilarity – with the relaxation of mind and spirit in God's presence which it brings. A chuckle can go a long way in making the truth memorable and acceptable; the absurd and risible can commend both preacher and message, and enhance the hearers' anticipation and appetite for the truth.

We should not fear, therefore, the light-hearted approach; neither should we feel that it is obligatory. The heart of the matter is that the Word of God is its own commendation. Think of 'the Bisto Kids' – or is that something only my generation know about? The advertisement for Bisto used to show the rich aroma of Bisto gravy wafting out from the kitchen, and the two ragamuffin 'kids' catching the scent and being irresistibly drawn home for dinner. The Bible is God's Bisto. It spreads its rich aroma; it creates appetite; it promotes hunger; it draws us in. The simple announcement of the 'text', the well-prepared reading of the passage, will, very often, prove to be the most powerful introduction.

As I look back over my notes I see that more and more I have adopted this approach. Nothing more is needed by way of 'introduction'. The Bible has done its work; the hearers are already 'with you' around this Word of God. But remember how individual the work of preaching is: we must each discover what 'works' for us.

Another approach along the same lines is to invite your congregation to 'take up an attitude of prayer while we hear the Word of God together', and, while every head is bowed, to read the verse or passage for the day, and then turn it into prayer and praise. Such a prayer needs to be well prepared ahead of time – but, then, so does any public prayer. But prayerful meditation on the Scriptures in this way is a delightful preparation both for the preacher and the hearer.

The Middle: Deadly Questions

I suppose some people are so overflowing with material that they are never plagued by the question 'Whatever am I going to say?' I don't know whether to envy them or not! I suppose it makes life easy, but 'never being short of something to say' could also mean 'never having anything worthwhile to say'. Our spontaneous overflow is not necessarily to be trusted or valued – as my first senior would put it: 'trying to glorify God with the rinsings of our minds'!

But the question 'what am I to say?' is a killer, and it is the wrong question. Ask rather, 'What does the Bible say?', for everything in the Bible is the Word of God, and God can make everything in His Word a blessing to His people. I remember listening to a conversation on the return journey from an evening service. The preacher had preached very acceptably – indeed, strongly and searchingly and with great liberty – on Psalm 23, and a third party was offering a word of appreciation. The preacher said, 'I'm more than grateful to you for that, because I had no real certainty that Psalm 23 was, in any particular way, the word for tonight.' 'How then,' said the third party, 'did you preach it with such conviction?' 'Oh,' said the preacher, 'because everything in the Bible is always God's Word for His people.' What a proper and practical attitude – first, to the Bible as indeed God's Word, and secondly, to the Lord who will always honour His Word and make it effective! Heavenly Bisto indeed!

Another deadly question which may well arise in the preacher's mind in the course of the preaching is 'Am I getting a response?' Believe me, this is one of Satan's tricks. I happen to think it is right to use sermons more than once. At the very least it is more honour to divine truth to make second use of a well-prepared sermon than to offer a hurried, less than well-thought-out effort, scrabbled together against the clock merely to observe a prejudice against resurrecting an old friend. Of course, there is actually no such thing as a mere repeated use. There has been fresh preparation of the old outline, refurbishment and adaptation of content to the new situation. But sometimes, in the course of a second – or fifty-second – use of a sermon (two Sundays ago I preached a sermon which first saw light of day in 1963, and has been 'on parade' nineteen times since!) the mind recalls the responsiveness (or seeming responsiveness) of former congregations, maybe at particular points, and the insinuation of Satan comes 'You're not getting the same response, are you?' If one falls into this temptation, in comes an element of striving after response; a rebuking voice which accuses, 'you're not doing your job properly! Try harder!' Be very careful! 'Response' is not my business; it is the business of the Holy Spirit. As the old prayer says, God alone 'can order the unruly wills and affections of sinful men'. Yes, He does use His word to change people's minds. Like Lydia in Acts 16:14 who was listening and 'the Lord opened her heart to heed the things spoken by Paul'. On this occasion all Paul did was 'speak' – a very ordinary verb (*laleo*). Paul was 'chatting' the truth; God brought about the response and effected the transformation. This is not only the secret history of every conversion; it is the gracious work of God, honouring His holy Word whenever that Word is shared. Stick to your task, and leave God to His! Send Satan packing! Even while you are actually engaged in preaching, bring your spirit back from the brink, rest on God, trust His faithfulness to His truth, commend the response of the people to Him. Be at peace. 'Response' is His work. The question we preachers should constantly ask ourselves is not 'Am I getting a response?' But 'Am I being clear?' 'Am I making the truth plain?' 'It is required in stewards that one be found faithful' (1 Cor. 4:2). This is our faithfulness: to make biblical truth plain while resting on God's faithfulness to bring His truth home to the hearers. Paul put the matter with exact succinctness in 1 Corinthians 3:6-7, 'I planted, Apollos watered, but God gave the increase. So then neither he who plants is anything, nor he who waters, but God who gives the increase', lit., 'the increasing God', as if to say that 'giving the increase' is a divine attribute.

Making an Appeal

When Dr Billy Graham came to Harringay in London in 1954 and in the following years there was great searching of heart among many Bible-loving people about whether or not it was right to make an appeal, to encourage people to 'get up out of their seats', or to remain behind for an 'after -meeting'. There were many, many sensitive souls who really and truly believed that appeals and after-meetings were a usurpation of the work of the Holy Spirit. It is easy to see why they thought like that, for we have all been subjected to 'appeals' which were no more than evangelistic bullying – prolonged appeals, hymns sung over and over, calls to this and that section of the audience. No wonder that sort of thing was seen as usurping the work of the Holy Spirit, for (though I think Dr Graham was not guilty of it) such indeed it is. One full-time evangelist, of considerable fame at the time, was overheard saying to another, 'No one knows, like we do, the strain of always having to be successful.' One's heart goes out to him. How could anyone bear such a strain? But had he not heard of the Holy Spirit?

To return, however, to the matter of 'making an appeal'. Bible in hand, the proper reaction is 'why not?' In the New Testament we find that *the statement of the truth includes the appeal of the truth*. Would it be too fanciful to think that when the Lord Jesus asked 'Have you understood?' He was conducting a sort of 'after-meeting'? But look at Acts 2:36-38. In his sermon Peter had been explaining the events of the day of Pentecost – how they fitted into

Joel's scriptural forecast, what they meant for his hearers, what they taught about Jesus. He ends with an appeal: 'Therefore let all the house of Israel know ... Repent ... be baptized ...' Turn to Acts 3:19. Following the healing of the lame man, Peter has been explaining about the power of the name of Jesus, and he has brought guilt for the death of Jesus firmly home to roost on his hearers and their rulers (though, note with what gentleness he did it, v. 17). Then comes the 'appeal': 'Repent therefore ...' In Acts 13:40 it is not a call to repent but a word of serious caution: 'Beware'. And in Paul's marvellous address to the Ephesian elders we find, 'Take care of yourselves' (Acts 20:28) and 'keep on the alert' (v. 31).

Endings

There are two major factors to be kept in mind, then, in bringing a sermon to an end: first, the task of creating and implementing a response is *totally the work of the Holy Spirit and must be left to Him*. But secondly, as it was stated above, *the statement of the truth* (the task granted to the preacher) *includes the appeal of the truth*. We are called to be faithful (to our task) and believing (in the Lord the Spirit). This calls for great sensitivity. It does not call for stopping short of the appeal which in any given text or passage is part of the truth of that passage – *the Word of God not only teaches what is true but also how to respond to what is true*.

Philippians 2:13, 14

This is a hugely important principle. Think about it: left to ourselves, we would neither know the truth or know what to do about it! The logic of the natural man and the logic of Holy Scripture are two separate things. Take, for example, Philippians 2:13. It is quite clear that in the matter of our sanctification God is the sole and total Agent. He is, as we could translate it, 'the one constantly and effectively at work': the verb here is a present participle, expressing a changeless attribute of that person. The verb (*energeo*) has the force of 'work effectively'. Furthermore, His work covers, in us, both the aspect of 'wanting' and 'willing' and the aspect of 'achieving', 'effectively accomplishing' (*energeo* again). Obviously, then, there is nothing left for me to do. He is the sole Doer. In this way logic would lead us into some notion of effortless sanctification, 'Let go and let God' with a vengeance! Not according to verse 14 with its command 'do all things'. Far from God's total activity negating our active commitment, it is actually what makes it possible and productive! This is but one example of what in fact happens throughout the Bible. There is a revelation both of what is true and also what to do about what is true. There is revealed truth and revealed response.

Returning, therefore, to preaching: if our response to the truth is part of what is revealed in any given passage, then our fidelity to Scripture requires us to bring that message, that appeal for action, to our hearers. This does not call for lack of passion and urgency in the preacher, as if our longing to see a response was in itself a trespass against the Holy Ghost. And yet … and yet … without doubt our appeals can so easily overstep the mark! Just remember: the declaration of the truth is our responsibility. This includes the truth about making a response, but actually promoting that response is His work.

A Preacher's 'Quadrilateral'
In 1 Thessalonians 1:5 Paul shares with us the four outstanding aspects, as he remembered them, of his

preaching ministry in Thessalonica – 'in word … in power … in the Holy Spirit … in much assurance.'

- 'Word' points to the basis of his preaching in the Word of God and the gospel of Christ, and also to the care which he took over the words he used and the clarity of his proclamation. Note the emphasis the negative statement provides – 'not in word only' as though to say, 'The Word, of course. Take that for granted'. That was where the whole work started. That is basic, the sharing of truth divine, the 'Word'.

- 'Power' speaks of Paul's awareness that something effective was happening. There was power at work in the Word.

- 'The Holy Spirit'. There are so many different sorts of 'power'. 'Mass hysteria' is one, and it has been shamefully exploited by unthinking preachers. Emotion is a very potent force too, as is the pressure of the prolonged, over-intense 'appeal'. It is for this reason that Paul was inspired to proceed by defining the sort of 'power' he meant, the power of the Holy Spirit at work, glorifying Jesus, illuminating minds, opening hearts.

- 'Much assurance'. Was the assurance something the preacher felt or something happening in the hearers? You will find the commentators swinging both ways, and offering persuasive reasons for doing so. Need we decide for one rather than the other? If the Word goes forth with the power of the Holy Spirit, the gracious Spirit is at work in the preacher as much as the hearer, surely. God's Word grips the speaker before it touches the hearer. There must be what Paul affirms about his ministry in Thessalonica.

The word must come 'in much assurance' (1 Thess. 1:5) – the confidence of the preacher in his message – if the same assured conviction is to be shared with others. The Word is both our message and our conviction; just as the Word is both what is heard and what is believed. If it does not burn us it will not burn anyone else! 'Passionless preaching' is a contradiction in terms. It is part of our personal preparation to bring the truth to bear on ourselves, to feel its pressures, to enter into its glories, to fall on our faces before its wonder. And then to rely on the Holy Spirit to impart a like assurance to those to whom we speak.

Look at this quadrilateral in terms of our old friend, an *inclusio*.

- From the hearer's point of view, the brackets are on one side the Word heard with clarity, and on the other side the Word believed with conviction. And the bracket encloses the Holy Spirit working with power. This is the context in which we preach: God graciously annexes the power of the Holy Spirit to the truth of His Word to produce results He desires.

- From the point of view of the preacher, the brackets are to proclaim the Word with clarity, and to do so with full assurance, and, within those brackets, to leave it to the Holy Spirit to work with power, because that is the 'mechanism' God has intended and which He blesses and uses.

Part of the Preparation

But the appeal is not the only way to end a sermon, is it? Here again sameness is tiresome. I think of a valued friend, who is also a fine preacher, but his almost invariable ending is 'God grant', and back we go over the salient points of the sermon with the prayer that God will grant whatever is appropriate to this or that truth. 'God grant' this, and 'God grant' that. Well, it is one way to end a sermon, and a good way at that – but every time? One can only assume that when it came to ending his sermons he relied on the inspiration of the moment rather than preparing in advance, and 'inspiration' was not necessarily there!

But the 'God grant' ending illustrates one very helpful way of bringing our sermons to a close: a deliberate summary. This is specially appropriate to teaching sermons: 'Very well, then, what have we learned ... First ... Second ... Third ...' The principle to follow is that the ending must match the sermon, i.e., it must be faithful to the truth which has been shared, and appropriate in 'enforcing' that truth; that is, bringing it home to our hearers. A teaching sermon ends with a summary; a 'practical' sermon (e.g., a sermon about prayer, Bible reading, evangelism) ends with suggestions of what to do next. If you are in the habit of beginning and ending your sermons with a call to prayer, do please remember to prepare what you are going to say in prayer, lest your prayer ramble on and the point of the sermon be lost in transit! Unprepared prayer is as great a menace as unprepared sermons!

Evangelism

The 'evangelist' has an honoured and high place among the stated gifts of the Holy Spirit to the Church (Eph. 4:11), and this special gift, like all gifts, is dispensed by the Holy Spirit according to His will (1 Cor. 12:11). Praise God for those who have been blessed with the gifts of the evangelist, and praise God that He sent them across our paths to be our midwives unto Christ. I am privileged to honour and love the name of Harold Wildish, a dear man of God and an evangelist to his fingertips. The Lord of the harvest brought him, from his work among the Assemblies in the Caribbean, to Dublin in 1940 to point me to Christ and to usher me, so gently, into the kingdom of the redeemed. And you will have, in the same way, a name or names on your roll of honour. Such men and women have been granted by God a special facility in presenting the truth of salvation, and in issuing the gospel invitation.

It is a beautiful gift of the Spirit but, again, like all the gifts, it is not for everybody, only for those to whom it is given. What, then, of the rest of us? I write as one who does not have the gift of the evangelist. Does this excuse me from evangelism? When I worked in a college, it was my duty to take my turn in leading 'college missions', and when I was privileged to serve in local churches I felt obliged to conduct evangelistic services. How is a person like me placed? Obligation without gift! I was greatly helped by what a colleague said to me – and though at first sight what he said may seem an exaggeration, it is not so. It is one way – and a very true way – of facing the facts and the obligations. He said, 'There is no such thing as an "evangelistic sermon", there is only the sermon which expounds evangelistic passages of the Bible.' What a relief! How very observant! We all have, in our minds, in an undefined way, what we think an 'evangelistic sermon' is, and, for myself, the realistic reaction is, 'No, that's not me. I couldn't compose or preach a sermon like that!' No, maybe not, but I can take those passages of the Bible where the evangelistic message is particularly plain and expound them, and let them 'run out' into whatever ending, including the evangelistic appeal, they demand. Yes, and so can you, and, like all the rest of the Word of God, this will reach its hearers in the power of the Holy Spirit and with full assurance.

Incidentals

Illustrations in a sermon don't help me, and I have to keep reminding myself that they do help other people, and must therefore be thoughtfully used. When listening to a sermon, if I sense an illustration coming on, I want to call out to the preacher, 'Yes, yes, we know all that. Please get on with the job!' But I know that my attitude has been formed by enforced listening regularly to a (very kindly and effective) preacher who abounded in what he called 'little stories'. They were of the variety 'In my last church but one, a lady came to me ...' – and as far as I was concerned I was already, at that early point, a disenchanted listener! I fear I can be inwardly very impatient. But, as far as your 'little stories' are concerned, I would suggest two things: first, make them short and snappy; and secondly, they will usually prove more effective if you tell them as though they happened to someone else ('I happened to be there when someone came up to a minister ...'). We don't want to put ourselves centre stage; the pulpit itself is danger enough. Possibly, for some, I should add, beware of a surfeit of illustrations: your hearers may start listening out for the stories and forget the sermon and, indeed, they may even remember the stories and forget the point they were meant to illustrate.

To tell you the truth, I have come to the conclusion that the chief usefulness of illustrations is to give our hearers a little rest! In fact, I find that – certainly nowadays – when I produce one of my limited selection of illustrations (usually some nonsense about one or other of my mildly eccentric aunts) I introduce it by saying; 'Have a rest. I've told you before about my Aunt Polly – indeed I fear I may have told you this before ...' And then get back quickly on track. But never use an illustration as a replacement for making the truth clear. Aim at such crystal clarity in words, arguments, teaching, presentation that if you do use an illustration it comes not as a necessity but as a bonus.

Stand still

The other 'incidental' I want to include here under the general heading of 'application', bringing the Word home to the hearer, is gestures – the waving arm, the pointing finger, whatever. People don't like listening to talking windmills. I find my arms start waving about either because that precious and covetable accompaniment to preaching, nervousness, has got out of hand, or because I have not prepared sufficiently thoroughly and am not 'master of my brief'. One preacher of my acquaintance – who saw more fruit for his ministry than ever I have done – much given to nervous jerks, upraised arms, hands sweeping backwards and forwards, and so on, was met at the door by a (very daring) member of his church, who said. 'Good sermon, Rector. Thank you so much. But as far as I could see this morning, it was 57 for 2, including four sixes, three no-balls and a couple of leg byes.' Like alliteration, gesturing can take our hearers' minds off the matter in hand. More about nervousness in the next chapter, but gestures can at least be moderated by holding your Bible in one hand or with both hands, and this is a good thing in its own right; it is what we are for: the open book is a picture of our function. It's all a matter of balance and proportion. A motionless preacher gives the impression of not being personally 'caught up' in the wonder, excitement, heat of the message – and that will never do. There's nothing wrong with the upraised finger pointing to the Throne, the downward gesture of the hand that drives a point home, the outspread arms accompanying an invitation. If the truth does not burn us up it will scarcely ignite anyone else. Just be careful and thoughtful; when we are called to preach, we are called to be at that moment the focus of all eyes. People are looking at us; make sure that neither by slovenliness of dress, nor by intrusiveness of action, nor by ill-preparedness of speech, they find the sight distracting. The scintillating Dr Willoughby, preaching at St Luke Hampstead, around the time of the First World War, used to get so caught up in his message that he started marking time on the spot and slowly gyrating a full 360 degrees back to where he started. People learned to watch out for this parade-ground manoeuvre, and half of them to dissolve into uncontrollable giggles, while the great man, remaining blissfully unaware of the spectacle he was creating, preached serenely on!

Task and Trust

'Jeremiah, what do you see?' said the Lord, and Jeremiah replied, 'I see the branch of an almond tree' (1:11) – a highly uninformative reply for a non-gardener like me who would not know an almond branch if he saw it! But, rushing to my aid, come the commentators. The almond was the first plant where signs of growth and of the advent of spring appeared. So I am told. Waxing poetical, the commentaries say it was the place where the iron grip of winter was seen to be broken. If that sounds dramatic, it is no more dramatic than the reality in our own gardens, when suddenly the dormancy and deadness of the winter months fall victim to the tiniest green shoot, where the brittleness of the winter twig is suddenly, and then gradually, green and pliant. Well, probably so for Jeremiah and the almond tree! Who am I to argue? In any case, this is the message the Lord used the almond branch to illustrate. In Hebrew an 'almond branch' is *shaqed* ('the waking one'), and the Lord responds by saying 'I am *shoqed* – on the watch/wide awake – over my word to do it.' The branch contains the principle of 'awakening' – an awakening powerful enough to break winter's grip – and the Lord matches that by His own alertness to implement the quickening power of His Word.

Our task is the Word; His task is the quickening.

Chapter 12

Behind the Scenes: Spirituality

Have you ever met a minister so caught up with the trappings and functions of office that you thought, 'I expect he (or, in these days, she) has a clerical collar he wears with his pyjamas'? The person submerged in the role? Before you laugh, it can happen with preachers too! John Mortimer, in one of his books, has a bishop whose every contribution to a conversation was automatically cast in the form of an incipient 'Thought for the Day' which he will later use on the BBC. The man had disappeared and the function had taken over. The 'mask' had increased; the person had diminished.

Paul

Acts 18 is very instructive – and rebuking and challenging. Paul did not wait for Silas and Timothy in Athens, but pressed on alone to Corinth. There, he first worked in partnership with a Jewish couple named Aquila and Priscilla, earning his living as a tentmaker, while at the same time 'reasoning' in the synagogue But by the time Silas and Timothy caught up with him, they found Paul 'devoting himself exclusively' (v. 5, NIV) to the ministry of the Word: Paul the indefatigable! He never stopped. Let his body be bruised and bleeding from a near lynching, but then show him a crowd and immediately he wants to preach to them (Acts 21:39). Flog and imprison him at Philippi, and he is 'emboldened' to preach at Thessalonica (1 Thess. 2:2). Give him a stadium filled with an angry crowd in an ugly mood, and he can just about be stopped from 'venturing' in (Acts 19:30-31). There is no need to labour a point so patently obvious. If ever a man was caught up in his ministry it was Paul; it was in every sense his life, so that he was even ready to postpone being with Christ, which is by far the best, for the immediate good of his Philippians and the envisaged fruit of his work (Phil. 1:21).

But look now at Acts 18:18 –

'He had his hair cut off at Cenchrea, for he had taken a vow.' (NKJV)

In a word, Paul had not forgotten his own personal walk with God, his own duty of consecration and devotion, expressed here in terms of the Nazirite vow of Numbers 6:1-8. Absorbed as he was in ministry, he was also committed to being himself 'holy to the Lord'. The details of his 'vow' are not revealed – my guess is that he consecrated himself to a special time of prayer and personal walking with God for the conversion of Aquila and Priscilla, who, in contrast to being 'Jews' in Acts 18:2 are now Paul's fellow travellers (v. 18) and one with him in Christ. But it doesn't matter. We are only told what we need to know: our 'vows' will not be the same as his, but in the thick of ministry let us be, as he was, those who are intent on our own consecration and our personal walk with God, setting aside time – including extended periods of time – especially for Him.

A dear friend, ministering in the far north of Scotland, spoke frankly of his early days in ministry – and how exactly they chimed in with mine, and, I believe, with many! In full-time ministry, he was at last where he had long wanted to be, following the call of God, at work in a local church. 'How I remember,' he said, 'spending the late hours on Saturday evening desperately trying to get right with God in time for Sunday.' Have you been there? It's the great snare of ministry, and, in my opinion, the outstanding failing of many a minister, to sacrifice the best in the interest of the good. Good? What indeed could be 'more good' than ministry to God's people, being up to our necks in the privileges, demands and exercises of the care of souls? Isn't this our calling, our duty, and our devotion? Of course! But at the cost of ceasing to be individuals saved by grace? Do we call others to daily prayer and forget our own prayers? Are we all out for the Word of God in the pulpit and forgetful of it as our personal 'means of grace' in the secret place? Yes, indeed, it is a horrible possibility – 'they made me keeper of the vineyards', but 'my own vineyard I have not kept!' (Song 1:6, ESV).

Ezekiel
Of all the prophets, Ezekiel gives us the longest account of his 'call': Ezekiel 1:1 to 3:27 (and very likely on to 6:14).

Not so much a 'call', we might say, as a term or two in the Lord's training school!

- Where does Ezekiel's 'schooling' start? The Lord came to him in the glorious and overwhelming self-revelation of Ezekiel 1, and, (v. 28) very understandably, the mere 'son of man', Ezekiel, fell on his face in the presence of that majesty – a correct reaction, surely, but the Lord had a further wish: 'Son of man, stand on your feet, and I will speak to you' (2:1). The Holy Spirit then came to Ezekiel (2:2) to enable him to stand before the Lord, and to hear Him speak. The priority, ahead of 'the Lord's work' and 'the Lord's people', is that the individual, called to that work and those people, should stand before the Lord (cf., 1 Kings 17:1) and hear Him speak.

- The Lord proceeded to present Ezekiel with the Word he was to minister (2:7–3:4). Ezekiel is commanded (v. 7) to 'speak my words'. Note that plural. The prophet's duty is to bring not, so to speak, the 'drift' or general impression of divine truth but the actual 'words' of the Lord. How can this be done? It is made possible by the gift of the written word (2:9–3:3). A fully written scroll – written on both sides, precluding the addition of anything by Ezekiel – is presented to the trainee prophet, and the section ends with the command (lit.,) to 'speak with (i.e., by means of/ by the instrumentality of) my words' (3:4). The Word is given; the Word is the *instrument* of ministry. The prophet is the person hearing God's Word, possessing God's Word, and sent to use that Word as the only needful tool in his ministerial kit. But Ezekiel must first 'eat' the Word given to him (3:1); indeed he must gorge himself on it (3:3). Further, sent to carry the Word to others, he must himself be the first to obey it – (2:8), 'Do not be rebellious like that rebellious house.' First to obey, and distinguished from all others by his obedience!

• The Lord's last word to Ezekiel in this central section of the call-narrative comes in 3:22-27. The Lord made His presence felt (the hand, v. 22), and He commanded Ezekiel to go out onto the plain, promising to speak to him there. If Ezekiel had replied, 'But you are speaking to me here! Why do I need to go there?', the Lord would (I believe) have said, 'No! You are the new man. The Holy Spirit has regenerated you (2:2). You must now exercise personal responsibility to be found in the place where the Lord's voice is to be heard.' It is in this setting – the prophet voluntarily, deliberately entering/being found in the place of hearing – that the ground rules of ministry are set out (v. 27): When I speak to you, you may speak to them.

In summary: the prophet devours the Word, obeys the Word, frequents the place where the Word is heard. Behind the public man lies his private, secret life with God in His Word: our Monday-to-Saturday and very early Sunday-morning personal habit. The public minister of the Word has to be fashioned in the secret workshop of the Word. The minister must never cease to be an 'ordinary believer' humbly walking with God in the light of His Word.

Standing at the Front, Sitting at the Back
We occupy the dangerous place that is ours in the public gaze, but we must only dare to do so as those who can say

with Elijah 'As the Lord, the God of Israel lives, before whom I have taken my stand and continue standing' (1 Kings 17:1) – the Hebrew perfect tense representing here both a deliberate action and an unchanging state. Publicly we stand up front, made prominent by pulpit or desk; privately, in heart, mind and attitude, we are sitting with all the rest, under the Word of God, open-eared, waiting, longing to hear what the Lord our God will say to us (Ps. 85:8).

Isaiah and the Lord's Servant

We now come to the highest ground of all. It fell to Isaiah to predict the coming of the Servant of the Lord, and, in this way, to let us into the secret of perfect service. Since we know that the messianic Servant whom Isaiah foresaw is our Lord Jesus Christ there is no holier ground in all the Old Testament for us than Isaiah 40–55, and, within those chapters, lies the Holy of Holies itself of the four Servant 'Songs' (42:1-4; 49:1-6; 50:4-9; 52:13–53:12).

Our concern here is with the third 'Song', the Servant in His distinct individuality, His holy obedience, the perfection of His discharge of the will of God – and the secret which underlay it all, the clue to Christlike discipleship.

The Lord GOD

Isaiah 50:4-9 is dominated by the fourfold occurrence of 'The Lord GOD' (vv. 4, 5, 7, 9), in each case given strong emphasis as the first word in its section. In most English versions, 'Lord' (the initial upper-case letter followed by three lower-case letters) is the Hebrew *adonai*, meaning 'master' and used of God in His divine sovereignty. 'GOD' (three upper-case letters), like the four upper-case 'LORD', represents the divine name, Yahweh, sadly treated by our translators as too holy to be expressed openly. The great subject of the Song is, therefore, Yahweh, the God of the Exodus (Exod. 3:15), the deliverer/redeemer God of Exodus 6:2-8 – in biblical terms, the God of all grace, the God of salvation – seen here as the all-sovereign: God who is God indeed, as if to say four times over, almost like a great exclamation to open each section: 'There is a Sovereign God. His Name is Yahweh!' In the second section (vv. 5-6), the Servant tells how He learned the will of God and committed Himself to doing it, no matter the cost; in the third section (vv. 7-8), resting on the help of the Sovereign Redeemer, He knows that He will come triumphantly through the ordeal of this obedient service, and in the fourth section, verse 9, still resting on sovereign help, He will see the end of every opponent.

Discipleship

So what, we may ask, is the secret of knowing the will of God (v. 5)? What is the secret of the presented body (vv. 6, 7, cf., Rom. 12:1), and of constancy in persevering in doing God's will? Where can one learn that simple but all-prevailing faith in God (vv. 7, 9) which carries the task through prevailingly, and with faith's assurance of ultimate triumph? The answer to all these questions lies in the opening section (v. 4), in what it says about 'discipleship'. The keyword comes twice. In verse 4, NKJV opts for the unfortunate and misleading translation 'the learned'. Literally, it is 'the tongue of those being instructed', i.e., 'disciples', those under instruction. Likewise, at the end of verse 4, 'as (is the case with) those being instructed'. The Servant of the Lord speaks of Himself as a disciple, actually numbering Himself in the company of disciples, making His discipleship the characteristic of all true discipleship.

These two references to 'disciples' mark off the two halves of the verse.

- The first half deals with the disciple's tongue: it is the gift of the Lord to know how to 'speak a word in season' – a lovely expression for an oft-felt longing – to have just that precise, right word which matches the situation and meets the needs of the listeners. How often we have muffed our chances, whether saying the wrong thing, or thinking too late what we ought to have said! Our uninstructed tongues (in sermons as well as conversations) are too often the cause of a sad 'if only' – 'if only I had thought to say …', 'if only I had said it differently!' How very important, therefore, to learn from the Perfect Disciple and Servant the secret of the instructed tongue!

- Without explanation, the Servant's testimony moves from His tongue (v. 4a) to His ear (v. 4b), but the link is surely obvious – namely, that those who want an instructed tongue must first seek to have an instructed ear. Indeed, what Isaiah says is even more important than the words 'want' and 'must seek' suggest. This is no mere human programme or matter of human wisdom; it is a revelation of the ways of God. The tongue is the Lord's gift; the opening of the ear is His work. This is how God does things. The tongue-ear nexus is something He has created. The ear open to what the Lord our God will say is (we may paraphrase, without too much violence to Isaiah's Hebrew) the hallmark of a disciple.

- The Lord who Himself, amazingly, wants to have this fellowship with His disciples ('he opens') also has an optimum time and an ongoing regularity: 'morning by morning'. I suppose – indeed I know – that there are those whose circumstances make the morning time impossible and who, therefore, must seek the permission of grace to substitute some other time for this privileged appointment. But the prophet was precise; he said 'morning by morning', the perfect Servant acted accordingly (Mark 1:35), and for the vast majority of us the morning time is possible, and, in the light of this passage, obligatory. Isaiah does not specify any particular hour or require any particular length of meeting – for what we used to call the 'quiet time'. Just the morning watch and the opened ear. Please allow me to be somewhat bold. I believe it cannot be right for us who have the privilege of 'full-time' ministry to enjoy our private devotions after the working day has begun for those to whom we minister – i.e., after 9.00 a.m – and when it should have begun for us too. That would be what Peter would call using our freedom as a 'cloak' for wrong (1 Pet. 2:16). We long to be like Jesus, do we not? Let us be like Him in the early morning!

- The central reality of the 'quiet time', this morning-by-morning meeting, is 'to hear'. In our terms, between the Lord who comes to meet with us and us who, Ezekiel-like, come to meet Him, lies the Word of God.

Discipleship, then, is characterized by daily fellowship with the Lord God centred on His Word. Out of that ongoing morning meeting comes the tongue equipped to speak the word in season, the mind that knows what the will of the Lord is, the will resolute to persevere through thick and thin, and the simple faith that rests confidently on His unfailing help. Like an inverted pyramid, a huge mass of blessings resting on one point: 'morning by morning he awakens my ear to hear'.

Satan the Activist

You will be familiar with the voice which nags you to be up and doing, to be out and about on the Lord's work. It is a voice some of us need more than others – me very much included – but it is also a voice to be tested, because it may be Satan at his ceaseless task of temptation. The devil does not mind how active we are in the work of the Lord provided we are achieving nothing, or, better still, falling flat on our faces. Therefore, he would gladly send us out unready, unequipped, unarmed into the fray. And, equally, it may be the Lord's good pleasure to turn the tables on the adversary by making our fumbling efforts in one way or another mighty for the gospel. We can only say, 'Be that as it may'. Since we try to be alert to Satan and his devices, we need to be clear-headed about this one. He would subvert the pattern set by the perfect Servant, encouraging us out into the field of battle when we have not first learned the habit and discipline of 'morning by morning'. May I remind you?

- It is there we learn the effective word, the 'word in season'. Dare we go out in ministry and in preaching without the word the Lord teaches?

- It is there we learn what is the Lord's will, as He opens our ears to hear. Those of you who have read Oswald

Chambers will have learned from that remarkable man that we need divine permission before we speak to anyone of Christ. In such a situation there is a divine 'match' between the word spoken and the person for whom it is designed. Who would not covet this to be the case? Isaiah teaches that it is the product of 'morning by morning'.

- It is there that we ourselves experience the transforming grace of God whereby we can remain consistent for the Lord, rock-like in the persistence and the steadiness His work demands. For just as the morning secret place bears the objective fruit of the word in season, so also it bears the subjective fruit of personal transformation – as the old hymn says, 'ere you leave the silence of that happy meeting place you will bear the shining image of your Saviour in your face'.[1] If that sounds a bit too easy, a slice of hymn-writer's licence, put it alongside the historical reality of the forty days and forty nights after which Moses' face (lit.,) 'beamed, because he talked with him' (Exod. 34:29).

Jesus told a parable (Luke 18:1-8) teaching that we should 'always pray and not lose heart'. For a long time I thought this meant that prayer guards us against collapse or faint-heartedness, or lack of resolve. The Lord's intention, of course, was rather to urge us to pray and not to lose heart in the task of praying, not 'give up halfway', to pray and keep on praying. Nevertheless, the Bible would have us know that praying people are durable people. Objectively, our prayers are heard, answered, and bring forth results.

---

1   From the hymn 'In the Secret of His Presence' (Ellen Goreh, 1883).

Subjectively, there is a 'kickback': prayer not only changes 'things'; it changes those who pray.

Gethsemane

There is a holier ground than even Isaiah walked. It can be put extraordinarily simply: in Gethsemane Jesus trembled, prayed, and never trembled again all through the ordeal of our salvation. The disciples failed to pray, and after that never stopped trembling! To keep alert and pray is to follow our Saviour and become like Him.

Chapter 13

The Last Lap

It seems to me that the key to an effective ministry is our own personal walk with God, our consistent closeness to Him or, as I once heard it put, 'We are blessed not for what we do but for the direction in which we are moving'. In other words, if we are constantly making our own spiritual progress, advancing in Christlikeness, growing in the grace and knowledge of our Lord Jesus Christ (2 Pet. 3:18), we will find that blessing follows. It is not the most able who are blessed in their ministry, but the most holy. I recall a colleague who, humanly speaking, had very little going for him as far as ministry was concerned. He had not been blessed with brains; he couldn't preach for toffee. Yet as I look back over his long ministry in four different places, I see a constant trail of blessing, of churches transformed and still growing to this day, of people drawn to Christ, of new ventures called into being and still flourishing. To the end he was still undersupplied with brains, still an indifferent preacher, but he was a man of transparent integrity who lived close to God. People could see it, and God blessed it.

The Pauline Principle

One of the key passages of the Bible to read, ponder, absorb – and to obey – is Paul's 'charge' to the Ephesian elders in Acts. 20:17-36. We have already used these verses to learn from Paul's own ministry of the Word of God. Now let us hear what he would counsel us as his successors in that ministry: (v. 28) 'Take heed to yourselves'. The verb (*prosecho*) is a strong one. NKJV rightly translates it 'beware' in Matthew 7:15; in 1 Timothy 3:8 it warns against being 'hooked' by alcohol; Hebrews 2:1 uses it of the close and persistent attention we should pay to foundational truths of the gospel. Imagine Paul counselling the elders to 'look after number one'! Yet that is what he does, and, of course, it makes sense. Apart from anything else, if we don't look after ourselves we won't be there to look after anyone else. But the deeper truth is that, wonderfully, if we care for our own vineyards the vineyard of the Lord will grow and bear fruit.

Nothing in ministry is all that easy, but everything is easier – easier to do, easier to bear, easier to endure – in the context of committed pursuit of holiness, daily nearness to God.

The Primary Duty and Work

The first duty of ministers is to pray for those to whom they are sent in ministry. I can't think of any one verse which commands this, but it could be inferred from Paul's example (e.g., Rom. 1:9; Eph. 1:16; Phil. 1:3, 4; Col. 1:3, 4, 9; 1 Thess. 1:2, 3; 2 Thess. 1:11). Rather than fuss over a word, why not just say 'a duty' or even a 'great duty' rather than the 'first duty', but my experience, such as it is, suggests that where prayer is put first, blessing follows hard behind. So then, as you contemplate preaching, pray for those to whom you are going. Lack of knowledge does not preclude prayer. Nowadays I often know few if any of those to whom I am sent, but the Lord knows them every one, and as I pray in broad, general terms, He can be relied on to fill in the names and details, and tick the boxes.

If the Lord has blessed you – as in former days, me – with full-time ministry, and Sunday-by-Sunday preaching in a local church, then the membership roll is our main prayer list, with, after our family, the first call on our time. I have no experience of mammoth-sized churches, but I do know that in a church growing in the 200s it is possible to pray for every member by name once a week, and for all the members by name in the early hours of Sunday morning. And what a difference it makes to Sunday ministry. To have been together at the Throne of Grace binds the people of God into one in a most unique and helpful way. If we love people before God in prayer, that spirit of love will be evident in our ministry, and will the more readily win its way into minds and hearts.

Earning the Right to be heard

Need I apologize for pursuing this line of thought a stage further? I think not, even though, in a way, I am going beyond my chosen 'Preaching? Simple teaching on simply preaching' brief.

133

Our position as ministers in a church gives us the right to preach, but it does not give us the right to be heard. I once attended service at a church where the minister was not only known as a skilled preacher, but also was widely in demand as a lecturer on pastoral work, pastoral care and pastoral problems – subjects which he handled with notable ability and helpfulness. I came from that service with a sense of unease which I could not at that time define, but, years later I had the chance to ask the minister in question how he found time, with his preaching and lecturing commitments all over the country, to engage in the pastoral care of his people. 'Oh,' he said, 'I do all my pastoral work in the pulpit.' Not in home visitation? Not in personal ministry to the sick and bereaved? Not in one-to-one counselling of the troubled? Only in the pulpit? My original unease suddenly had an explanation. I remembered my attendance at his church: he was preaching but no one was listening! It was the minister's Sunday performance before we all could go home! His position gave him the right to preach; but, Monday to Saturday, he was not purchasing the right to be heard.

Just as our prayers for those whom we serve are the product of our love for them, and also cultivate a context of love for our pulpit ministry, so – possibly to an even greater extent – does our 'care for souls', displayed in the home, at the fireside, by the bed, in the hospital, in wedding preparation, in baptismal classes, in preparation for church membership. The diligent pastor is the most welcome preacher.

Self-awareness
Turn now with me to the other side of the coin. We have been thinking about the people to whom we minister.

Now let us think for a bit about ourselves as we set out to minister.

In a team situation, the senior minister may have said, Will you preach on Sunday morning? Or the secretary of the local church may have come on the phone: Are you free for Sunday …? And the people expecting to attend worship may say, So-and-so is going to give the sermon. Each of these is true in its own way – I am here by human decision and appointment; I have been asked back to preach; I am going to 'give the sermon'. Each reflects the way a local church 'works', but none of them properly defines what I am, and what I am going to do, and why I set out to do it. Therefore, none of them offers a way by which I can properly prepare for the task ahead. And it is so important that I go to my work in the right 'mind'.

We are not preachers by human direction, or because this is one of the ways a church functions and which, therefore, must be organized, nor to fill a gap which would otherwise occur in the scheme of worship. None of these (necessary) things girds us for the work. It is the call of God, the sense of His permission and will, and, above all, the ministry of the Word of God that is our authorization to be in this work and to undertake this function. Put it this way: I am not the senior/assistant minister or the invited preacher 'giving a sermon'. I am charged with ministering God's Word; I am a minister of divine truth.

This is colossally important. In early days of inexperience, there can be 'who am I to do this?' In later days of greater experience, there can be the casualness that familiarity brings: We've been here before, done this many times. The superficiality of being an 'old hand'. The one thing that effectively sustains and gives authority to the novice, and that rebukes the 'can-do' mentality of the seasoned is the wonder, the awesomeness, the solemnity, that the Word of God has been entrusted to me for this occasion, for these people. Here lies a true ground of confidence where we might be unconfident; here is the true antidote to any and all superficiality. The preacher's true self-awareness is that of one charged with divine truth, entrusted with the Book of Books, responsible before God for human souls and their eternal welfare.

A Common Denominator

Wherever we find ourselves 'comfortable' in the catalogue of the servants of God, it is all the same. Do we identify most easily with the trembling Jeremiah, with the excitable, imaginative Ezekiel, or with the magisterial Isaiah? They all viewed their place and task in the same way.

Jeremiah and nervousness

Most of us will find Jeremiah the easiest of the prophets to identify with, as far as the exercise of ministry is concerned. When he said 'I cannot speak, for I am a youth', which of us has not been there? And which of us has never wanted to sidestep the will of God through nervousness and the reality of personal inadequacy? But it was precisely as that nervous, inadequate-feeling individual that the Lord sent him to the work! Look at Jeremiah 1:17 and 18. One verse (17) commands Jeremiah not to be 'dismayed' (lit., 'shattered', i.e. by fear, nervousness, etc.), and consequently therefore his nervousness remains; the next verse (18) promises ability to stand up against all the enemy can throw at him. Keeping the two verses together, Jeremiah the nervous is called to act in faith that the Lord will make him sufficient for the task. Nervousness remains; faith obeys. And that's the way the Lord's work is done. In whatever way we feel inadequate we are called to act in 'the obedience of faith'. Nervousness would say 'I can't, therefore I won't'. The obedience of faith says 'I can't, but He can, so I will'. Therefore, never pray to be delivered from nervousness. Apart from anything else, it keeps us from ungodly self-sufficiency; it keeps us cast on the Lord. Our calling is never just obedience, always the obedience of faith.

Ezekiel and responsibility

In the course of his time in the Lord's training school, Ezekiel was alerted to the responsibility he bore as the Lord's 'watchman' (3:16-21). This is such an awesome thing that I dare do no more than call attention to it. Failure to issue the Lord's warnings – whether to the 'wicked' or to the lapsed 'righteous' – brings blood-guiltiness on the head of the watchman. Such responsibility for the eternal welfare of souls is more than we can bear. It is important to note that our task is to make the truth clear, to let people know where they stand. Their response is not our business, however much we are keen that they turn the right way. Remember also that 'to warn' is only one part of our concern as we go to preach and teach God's truth. We must neither forget the warning note, nor must we be obsessed with it. Balance is everything. But looking candidly at Ezekiel's position as watchman, and also broadening its implications to cover all our ministry of the Word, what a responsibility is ours.

Isaiah and the point of no return

At first sight, Isaiah, when he was called to be a prophet, received the strangest instruction – to command people not to understand – and the strangest task – to make the people impervious to his message (6:9, 10). This is actually what the Lord said to him, but, in order to understand it, we must ask how Isaiah set about obeying. The 'logical' way to obey would seem to be to make his message obscure and complicated, to set out to confuse and obfuscate, but, on the contrary, Isaiah spoke with such simplicity and crystal clarity that his opponents said his message was only fit for the kindergarten (28:9-10), not for the 'real world' in which politicians had to operate. He was a true preacher, making the Word of God plain beyond question. So we must look at it like this: the only way to break through inveterate hardness and opposition to the truth is to tell the truth all over again. Only the truth can overcome ignorance and the refusal of the truth. Isaiah knew this, and it determined how he acted. But, at the same time, to declare the truth once again is to risk yet another refusal, and, grimly, the very next refusal may provoke a final and irremediable heart-hardening. It may be the point of no return. Think about it. People experimenting with substance abuse never know ahead of time when the point of no return will be reached, and they will be 'hooked'. For one it may come with the first experiment; for others it will be further down the line. But the point of no return is there, waiting, and only God knows in advance – indeed, in His justice, has decided in advance – when it will come. So it was in the time of Moses: the moment of the irretrievable hardening of Pharaoh's heart had arrived; his probation was over; his disobedience to the call of Moses meant the die was cast. So also for Isaiah. The terms of his commission warned him that his message gave his people their final chance to listen. This was the moment when probation ended; one more declaration of the truth, one more chance to respond, or, alternatively, another refusal would be the final refusal.

What a solemn thing it is to preach the Word of God. Eternal destinies lie in the hands of the preacher.

The Prayer of the Preacher
How else can we face our calling to preach except in the spirit and practice of constant, earnest prayer: that the Lord will give us (like Jeremiah) the spirit of faith to rest – in all our hesitations, nervousnesses and fears – on His promise of sufficiency; that (with Ezekiel) He will make us faithful in dealing with souls, faithful to teach and to warn; and that (with Isaiah) He will keep us sensitive to the eternal issues at stake and graciously work to guard every one of our hearers from the dreadful pit of refusal of His Word.

Prayer has another function as well, as the final step in our preparation of the particular message with which we are charged.

I am taking for granted the 'memory' aspect of final preparation. Whatever we take with us the into the pulpit, be it a full manuscript, a manuscript with salient points underlined or highlighted, or a note of headings and points, our basic situation should be that we do not actually need any of these aids. The message is firmly gripped in mind and memory. But, beyond this, there is something specially helpful with which to conclude our preparation for the pulpit, and that is to pray our way through the forthcoming sermon, taking each section and each sentence in turn. To start with a prayer that the Lord will grip the attention of the listeners, a prayer for the opening, for help over foreseeably difficult places; praise too for the wonder of the truths that are shared; prayer that at each point of the sermon our demeanour may commend the message. Just soak the whole enterprise in prayer, praise, thanksgiving and intercession. Such prayer 'works backwards', fitting the preacher for the task, 'outwards', creating hearing ears in the listeners, and 'upwards', longing for the glory of the Lord.

Chapter 14

The Tenderest Word of All

If you have persevered with me to this point, then may I plead for the tiniest further extension of your attention – just a final word in your ear.

I have heard it said that in every sermon there should be enough 'gospel' to save some listening sinner. No one could possibly question the motive behind such a suggestion. It is simply 'apostolic'. In 1 Corinthians 9, Paul first (vv. 1-3) affirms that he is an apostle and then goes on to tell us how he lived out his apostleship – how he had every right to church support (vv. 4-12) but refused to claim his rights (vv. 13-18), choosing rather to go out of his way to identify with all conditions and classes of people (vv. 19-23), and ready to face the costliness of such a life in personal self-discipline (vv. 24-27). Look especially at verses 19 and 22-23, the bracketing verses round the key section on 'getting alongside' those to whom we minister. One motive governed all – verse 19, 'that I might win the more'; verses 22-23, 'that I might by all means save some'. No ministers cast in the apostolic mould would want to distance themselves from this great ideal of what used to be called 'soul-winning'. No indeed! God forbid that we should ever lose sight of the sinner's need of the Saviour, or cease to feel some serious identification with Paul in his 'heart's desire and prayer to God … that they may be saved' (Rom. 10:1). But, as I believe, this objective can be met in more ways than one.

Christ in all the Scriptures

First, we must ever keep in mind (a truth earlier chapters have already emphasized) that our task as preachers is to be faithful to the Scriptures, and that results are the work and business of the Holy Spirit. This means that if the evangelistic message is not inherent in the Scripture being handled, it would be a misuse of our stewardship to force it in. Always our entrustment is intense faithfulness to whatever verse or passage lies before us – but always explicitly praying that the Lord will do His own work and that it may please Him to bring the unsaved to salvation.

Doubtless, by divine mercy, this is something that has happened over and over again as the Word has been faithfully presented, but let me share one example. A minister returned from expounding Scripture at a Bible rally in a town hall in Wiltshire. It was a meeting designed for Christians, and his subject (Ps. 95) did not include, on that occasion, what we would call the evangelistic gospel. The thrust of the exposition was the call to obedience to

God's Word that is so plain in that psalm. Yet, that night – frankly to the expressed astonishment of the preacher – a man was converted.

The great, encouraging and reassuring truth expressed in this single instance is that Christ <u>is</u> in all the Scriptures, and, in that basic sense, every preaching of Scripture is a preaching of Christ. Because that minister was faithful to the passage in hand, he was, all unknowingly, a vital link in the work of the Holy Spirit in bringing a sinner to salvation. Neither in fact nor in intention was he 'preaching the gospel', but 'faith comes by hearing, and hearing by the Word of God' (Rom. 10:17). The Word was faithfully presented, and the Holy Spirit worked the miracle of hearing and gave the heaven-sent gift of faith.

'Christ … the Hope of Glory … Him we preach' (Col. 1:27, 28)

Preaching from the Old Testament, said a dear friend, is like going hunting with a double-barrelled gun. You fire off the truth from the Old Testament and apply it from the New! Well – provided, like all illustrations, we don't over-press details – the truth is there. There is a wonderful potency in the way the Lord Jesus steps off the page of the Bible as He knew and loved it, and then allows us to turn to the fully drawn portrait in the completed Scriptures. May I, as a non-gardener, take my life in my hands and attempt a horticultural illustration? Think of a perennial plant. In its first year, all the reality of the plant is present, yet it is but a preliminary expression of the flowering of the plant when it comes to its full maturity. So, in what we call the Old Testament, we have all the reality of what is yet to be, yet it is but a 'shadow' of the 'very image' or 'substance' yet to come in Christ (Col. 2:17; Heb. 10:1). But what richness, what fullness, when 'shadow' and 'substance' are brought together! So it was on the Gaza road when the Ethiopian invited Philip to sit with him in his chariot, and when Philip 'opened his mouth, and beginning at this Scripture, preached Jesus to him' (Acts 8:35). Do you wonder the man was converted that day? The whole power of shadow and substance was brought to bear on him, the transformative energy of God's completed truth. And the same power will prove its reality in our ministry when we perform the like service for those to whom we are sent, as we begin 'at Moses and all the prophets' and expound 'in all the Scriptures the things concerning' Him who is the grand and dominant Subject of the Bible from end to end (Luke 24:27).

Where the Light Falls

When John turned to see the voice that spoke to him he 'saw seven golden lampstands' (Rev. 1:12). Remarkably, they were not designed to shine the light of God's truth into the darkness of the surrounding world – though doubtless they did that as a by-product of their golden radiance. No, their lamps were turned inward in order to reveal the presence and glory, at their centre, of 'One like the Son of Man' (v. 13).

One way or another this expresses our intention and longing as preachers – that He should be at the centre, ever the Focus of all truth and fully illuminated for every eye, for 'we do not preach ourselves, but Christ Jesus the Lord', that all may see 'the light of the knowledge of the glory of God in the face of Jesus Christ' (2 Cor. 4:5-6).

Appendix 1

A Thought a Day for Six Days on

Death and Heaven for the Christian

DAY 1
Read Genesis 25:8; 2 Samuel 12:23; Psalm 73:23, 24:

Glory
We usually think of death simply as 'the end', the end of life, but the Bible does not: as these Old Testament verses show, right from the earliest times, the Bible insists that the dead live on. Abraham is 'gathered to his people': they have gone before him and await him; he joins them, just as David looks forward to joining his dead infant son. This is a lovely thought for us: we will join the whole people of God and our own dear ones who have died in Christ. The psalm tells us that this is to be seen as going 'into glory' and that it is something the Lord does for us – He 'takes' us to glory (see NIV).

DAY 2
Read John 10:28, 29; 2 Corinthians 5:1; Colossians 1:12, 13:

Assurance

Can we be certain? The words of Jesus are <u>very</u> reassuring: no one can pluck His sheep out of His hand. Paul carries this assurance on in 2 Corinthians: emphasise the verb 'we *have* a house not made with hands, eternal, in the heavens.' And when you read the Colossians verse pay very particular attention to the past tense: the Father Himself '*has* qualified' us. As far as <u>He</u> is concerned, we have been fully ready for heaven ever since we first trusted in Jesus for salvation.

DAY 3
Read Philippians 1:23; Luke 23:43:

What happens?

It is proper that we should want to know what happens when we die. Death is such a complete break with all that is familiar that we naturally feel frightened. Where will we be? How will it feel? What a blessing that these questions are basically answered by the highest and dearest authority of all – our Lord Jesus Himself. 'Today you will be with me in Paradise.' The verse speaks of an immediate experience following death (today); it speaks of personal survival and consciousness ('you'); it speaks of companionship and guardian care ('with me') and it speaks of that glorious place which God has prepared for His people ('in Paradise'). To Paul this was (literally) 'better by far' than anything earth could afford.

DAY 4
Read Revelation 7:9-17:

Guardian Care, Full Provision
This is a longer passage than for earlier days, but what a passage! Once we start reading we don't want to stop. If it were not in the Bible it would be too good to be true. Since it is in God's book, it is too good not to be true. Verse 9 describes the eternal companionship the Lord's people have with each other and with the Lamb (Jesus); verses 10-12 describe joy issuing in praise; verses 13, 14 tell us the one thing this great and diverse company all have in common: each has been cleansed in the blood of Jesus; verses 15-17 show how we will be eternally welcomed home into His tent; verse 16, eternally protected; verse 17, eternally provided and eternally comforted.

DAY 5
Read Philippians 3:20, 21; 1 Thessalonians 4:16, 17:

The consummation when He comes
When we die, our 'souls' go to be with Christ but our bodies remain and receive the last loving duties from our families and friends. But the Lord's plan is that every bit of us, bodies as well as souls, will be rescued from darkness, decay and corruption. This will happen when Jesus comes again, and both those who are alive and those who have previously died will be gathered together into His presence and He 'will change the bodies of our humiliation and make them like the body of His glory.' Then, indeed, we shall be complete – and completely like Him.

DAY 6
Read John 14:1-3: 17:24:

Our home prepared with Jesus

How good to end our thoughts with the very words of Jesus. See how, in 17:24, He makes His will. It is His will to bequeath to us a share in His glory. We can't imagine it but we must try to do so: He has willed that we will be with Him and see His glory. That is where we are going: to that loveliest of all companionships, that brightest of all visions. But John 14:1-3 makes it all homely and manageable: He has prepared rooms for us in His Father's spacious house and it is His personal task and intention to come personally to usher us into the heavenly place where He is. He will do this finally and dramatically when He comes again, but does He not also mean that He comes individually for each one of us to see us safely through death into the life which is life indeed?

Now, to whom is all this eternal blessing, happiness and security promised? John 14:1 records what *Jesus* said: You have put your trust in God; you have put your trust in me. That's all: Heaven's eternal blessings are ours by simply trusting Jesus.

Appendix 2

A Thought a Day for Six Days on

Our Task of Sharing the Gospel

DAY 1
Read Matthew 28:18-20

The Lord Jesus told us to share the gospel
There is nowhere in all the world where Jesus is not Lord: He has 'all authority in heaven and earth'. When we are fearful of going to a friend's house feeling that we ought to speak about Jesus, we need to remember that He is Lord even there; or when we fear what someone's reaction might be – Jesus is Lord over that too! And, of course, we never go alone: the promise of His companionship is given to those who go and tell others about Him (v. 20). But the very heart of this little passage is that when He came back from the dead He left us this command to go and tell.

DAY 2
Read Ephesians 2:11-13

People need us to tell them about Jesus
What do these verses say about people who are 'separate from Christ'? They know nothing of heart-warming friendship and fellowship (excluded from citizenship); they have no lovely promises of God to comfort and uphold them (strangers to the ... promise); they have no hope of heaven to look forward to (without hope) and they are estranged from God Himself (without God). What a plight! And all this can be remedied if and when they are 'brought near through the blood of Christ'. We are incredibly privileged: all these blessings are already ours and we must be careful to share them.

DAY 3
Read Acts 18:9-11

Jesus will help us in the task of sharing the gospel
It is comforting to know that Paul too was scared – otherwise why should Jesus tell him not to be afraid (v. 9)? But the Lord Jesus did not just tell him to get on with the task of speaking up; He added an assurance, 'I am with you'. We can picture the Lord Jesus speaking like this to Paul and then we can remind ourselves that He is 'the same yesterday, TODAY, and for ever' (Heb. 13:8). What He was to Paul, He is to us: the same in His commands (speak and do not be silent) and the same in His assurance (I am with you); and the same in His purpose to bring to Himself the 'many people' for whom He died.

DAY 4
Read Acts 8:32-35

It is not a complicated thing to share the good news
One of our fears always is that if we begin to talk to someone, we will soon get into deep waters, out of our depth
and not know what to say. There is always a perfectly good
answer to any question we might be asked: 'I don't know'
– and this gives us the opportunity (see John 9:12, 25)
to take the initiative and say something we do know. See
how Philip came straight to the point: he 'told him the
good news about Jesus' (v. 35, NIV). We can always have
a word prepared about what Jesus means to us, how He
cares for us, how He died for us, how He never forsakes
us, how He has a place prepared for us in heaven ... something we can share. No, sharing the good news may not be
easy, but it's not complicated.

DAY 5
Read Colossians 4:2-4

We must help each other by our prayers to share the good news
How are we to 'devote ourselves to prayer' (v. 2)? Someone
spoke the other day about his difficulty in spending long
periods in prayer but, as he said, reckoned that he 'nattered
to the Lord most times of the day'. How beautifully open
to our prayers the Lord Jesus is! And even Paul looked
for prayer support as he waited for God to open doors of
opportunity for him. We should pray that God will open
doors for us to share the good news and pray for each
other that, as opportunity offers, we may enter into it with
real clarity.

DAY 6
Read 2 Timothy 4:1-2

The Lord Jesus will ask us one day if we have shared the gospel
Don't you think that this title correctly sums up what Paul is saying to Timothy? One day the Lord Jesus will return. Naturally, He will want to ask us about how we used the time He gave us on earth – we remember the story of the noble man who, leaving home, gave money to his servants to trade with while he was gone; and when he returned as King he called them to give an account (Luke 19:11-26). We have been left with the treasure of the good news of Jesus Himself. His very last command to us was to share this news (see Day 1). It cannot but be the topic of His conversation with us when He returns. We don't want to be ashamed before Him at His coming!

Appendix 3

A Thought a Day for Six Days on

The Glory of Jesus in His Life

We beheld his glory. (John 1:14)

Sometimes in the gospel stories the glory of Jesus is actually mentioned (see Days 1 and 2, for example). Often the people's reaction to Him, their amazement and wonder, allows us to share that moment when something glorious about Him was displayed.

DAY 1
Read John 2: 1-11

Glory in Power and Provision
It is verse 11 which stakes the claim for this passage to be the first reading in a series on the glory of Jesus in His life, for this is where He chose to begin to display His glory.

It was in a very ordinary setting, a village wedding, for it is part of the grace of the Lord Jesus to come down into the everyday things of our lives. It was a moment of need: the provisions made did not meet the requirements of the guests. The need was met by something only God could do, for Jesus did not lay His hands on the water or indeed appear to do anything: He just made up His mind that this water should become wine, and so it was. All the power of God the Creator brought down to meet our common, ordinary need: that is the glory of Jesus.

DAY 2
Read John 11:1-16, 38-44

The glory of love, waiting and acting
Jesus Himself said (v. 4) that this incident would reveal His glory. Love was involved, for our Lord loved the trio in Bethany (v. 5). How odd, then, that He did not go running to be with them when He heard of their dire need. But no, because He loved them, He waited (v. 6). Just as we often question why He does not come quickly in answer to our cry, He doesn't, because He loves us and is working out a far greater purpose – for us and for Himself – than would be achieved by a quick response. But in His own time, He arrived and His arrival was well worth waiting for. The more we ponder the glory of Jesus as revealed in this story, the more we will be patient and trusting. His glory is the glory of a love which first waits and then acts.

DAY 3
Read Luke 4:14-22

The Glorious Teacher

One day they said about Jesus, 'No one ever spoke like this man' (John 7:46) and this was so right from the start, for in Luke 4 we listen to Jesus' first public utterance as Luke records His ministry – when they listened to His teaching (v. 15) all 'glorified' Him; when they heard what He said they were amazed (v. 22) at His gracious words. No wonder: He says one thing about Himself (v. 18a), how He has been richly endowed with the Spirit of God; then He goes on to tell of five things He has come to do for us – good news, freedom, sight, release, God's favour. We find ourselves in all sorts of poverty – of spirit, circumstances, pocket; bound by all sorts of forces too strong for us, by no means as open-eyed to God's truth and the loveliness of His Word as we would wish in our better moments. Jesus is always the answer.

DAY 4
Read Mark 7:31-37

Amazing Glory: the truly gentle touch

People were overwhelmed with amazement (v. 37) at what Jesus did. With great sensitivity He led the sufferer away from the crowd. Their shouts of astonishment would be far too much for newly awakened ears. By using sign language – His fingers, saliva, His eyes lifted to heaven – He communicated with the man in the only way his deafness allowed, as if to say: I am the healer; I heal by prayer. But notice, before the healing and before the man could hear, Jesus groaned. For before ever He takes away any disability, burden, care or need from us, He identifies Himself with our problems and groans beneath the weight of them.

DAY 5
Read Matthew 3:13-17

The Glory of the Man without sin
John the Baptist did not yet know that Jesus was the Messiah (see John 1:32-34), but Jesus was related to him (Luke 1:36) and already John knew something very wonderful about his cousin: this man, Jesus, had no need of baptism involving repentance and seeking the forgiveness of sins. Where others were confessing their sins as they stood in the water with John (v. 6), Jesus was speaking about 'righteousness' (v. 15) – what must be done in order to fulfil all God's righteous will and purposes. Look up Hebrews 7:26; 1 John 3:5; 1 Peter 2:22; 2 Corinthians 5:21. Jesus was utterly sinless.

DAY 6
Read Matthew 9:1-8

The Glory of God in the face of Jesus Christ
Jesus Himself said that whoever saw Him saw the Father (John 14:9). When the scribes complained that in forgiving sins Jesus was doing what God alone could do (v. 3, see Mark 2:7), He did not seek to avoid the implication that He was God, come to earth. He accepted that it was so and proceeded to give proof by restoring the man to health. So we, too, look at Jesus and see in His face the glory of God – this glory above all that as far as the east is from the west, so far He puts our sins from us (Ps. 103:12).

Appendix 4

A Thought a Day for Six Days on

The Church as the Bride of Christ

DAY 1
Read 2 Corinthians 11:2-4

Really Knowing Jesus
Paul had himself been to Corinth to tell the good news of Jesus and many people had become Christians. He sees this like becoming engaged (v. 2): we have pledged ourselves to Jesus, to be totally His. When He comes for us we want to be ready, pure for Him. But Satan is on the attack and his target is our minds (v. 3) – it is so easy to be led astray from the real Jesus and the true gospel (v. 4). It is part of our commitment to the Lord Jesus Christ that we should know the truth and hold onto it. This is why God has given us the Bible so that we can know the truth, become grounded in the truth and grow in the truth.

DAY 2
Read Ephesians 5:25-27

Becoming clean and staying clean
As a young man sets out to win a girl's love, so the Lord Jesus set out to win our love – by dying for us (v. 25). The effect of His death is described as 'the washing of water': just as water makes us clean, so does the blood of Jesus: He discharged our debt, bore our sins and our record is clean. And He has given us His 'word' that this is so (v. 26). He wants us to remain holy and unspotted (v. 27): this is our daily calling.

DAY 3
Read Revelation 19:6-8

The Wedding Day at last
The Book of Revelation has brought us here to the great Day when Jesus has come. God's great work of salvation is completed (v. 1); all His enemies are overthrown (v. 3) and the great crowd of the redeemed rejoice in heaven (v. 6). The joy is the joy of the Wedding Day (v. 7) and the bride is busy putting on her wedding dress (v. 8). Like all wedding dresses, it has taken some time to make. This one is very special because it is made up of the 'righteous deeds of the people of God'. Every time we live in the likeness of Christ, do what is right in His eyes, obey His commands, follow His will, we are sewing another stitch into the wedding dress in preparation for the glory of that Day.

DAY 4
Read Revelation 21:2-4

Joy unmarred
The city pictures the total company of the redeemed people of God, the citizens of New Jerusalem, the bride

of Christ (v. 2). Like every thoughtful bridegroom, this one has a home ready for His bride – His own tabernacle or tent where He Himself lives and where fellowship and mutual company will never again be broken (v. 3). Here on earth our loveliest occasions of human joy are often marked by sad tears – perhaps the list of wedding guests cannot be complete because death has taken away some valued member of the family. But at that wedding nothing can mar the happiness (v. 4).

DAY 5
Read Revelation 21:9-11

Who is she marrying?
Not just 'married' to Jesus but to 'the Lamb' – Jesus full of that special love for us that made Him ready to go all the way to Calvary, to the Cross for us, taking our place, bearing our sin, suffering all that we should have suffered, actually experiencing death for us so that we should have eternal life. The bride of such a Husband will need to be very special indeed. However could we be worthy of such an honour or make ourselves ready for such a Bridegroom? There is no need to worry. The bride is full of the most perfect glory (v. 11), but it is glory given by God Himself. Our salvation is all of God and He will see to it that we are fit to be united fully with His Son.

DAY 6
Read Revelation 21:22, 27

The Certificate has already been written out
When God's people lived in tents, His tent, the tabernacle, was pitched at the centre of their tents. The Lord came to live among His people. When they settled down in the

Promised Land and were living in houses, He allowed them to build Him a house, the Temple. This is the picture behind verse 22. We will live with Him where He is. Of course, of ourselves we would have no right to enter such a dwelling – the first half of verse 27 describes us all too accurately and leaves us in no doubt that we cannot come in. But the second half of verse 27 has a different story to tell. Jesus has a book in which are written the names of all those whom He died to save: it is true that by themselves they are unclean and all the rest of it but He, the Lamb, has died for them. His blood was shed for them. They have been cleansed by His precious blood. They can come in. Oh, what a blessing is ours! And it is all because of the Lord Jesus Christ.

> I promised you in marriage to one husband, to Christ, so that I might present you as a pure virgin to him. But I am afraid that just as the serpent deceived Eve by its cunning, your minds may somehow be led astray from your sincere and pure devotion to Christ. For if someone comes to you and preaches a Jesus other than the Jesus we preached ... (2 Cor. 11:2-4, NIV)

> (Husbands, love your wives, just as) Christ loved the church and gave himself up for her, to make her holy, cleansing her with the washing with water, through the word, in order to present her to himself as a glorious church, without stain or wrinkle or any other blemish, but that she should be holy and blameless. (Eph. 5:25-27)

Hallelujah!
For our Lord God Almighty reigns.
Let us rejoice and be glad
And give him glory!

For the wedding of the Lamb has come,
    And his bride has made herself ready.
Fine linen, bright and clean,
    Was given her to wear.

(Fine linen stands for the righteous acts of the saints.)
(Rev. 19:6-8)

Appendix 5

A Thought a Day for Six Days on

The Church as the Temple of God

DAY 1
Read Exodus 29:42-46

The Lord living among His people
The people of Israel had sheltered beneath the blood of the lamb (Exod. 12:13; 22, 23) and so had been brought safely out of their slavery and degradation in Egypt. The Lord had a lovely purpose in all this: 'so that I might dwell among them' (v. 46). Look at the diagram on page 166: they lived in their tents and, right at the centre of the encampment, the Lord had His tent pitched. He truly lived among them and met with them and spoke with them (v. 42), giving them a sure knowledge of Himself (v. 46). We do not have a visible tent or building marking the presence of the Lord

among us but the truth is the same: He is present for us to meet with Him and learn from His Word.

DAY 2
Read Ephesians 2:19-22

The building in course of construction
Once we were far off but we have been brought near to God by the blood of Jesus (v. 13) – just like stones are quarried at a distance and carried to the site and built one by one into the growing building. There is a huge cornerstone binding the building together so that it is all firm and secure: this is Jesus in whom we have our eternal security. But the building itself is designed to be God's Temple in which He will live. All that was once true in Exodus 29 (see day 1) is much, much more true for us. We do not just live around the building; we are the building and the Lord Himself – Father, Son and Holy Spirit (see how all Three are mentioned in the verses) – is among us.

DAY 3
Read 1 Corinthians 3:16, 17

You are the Temple
Of course the temple is holy. The Lord lives there. The Occupant sanctifies the house. Since we are the temple, we are called to be His holy people: the holy setting in which He lives. This obliges us to be holy in every way, in every part of our lives. But there is one special holiness which this passage has in mind. In verse 17, Paul warns against 'destroying the temple', that is pulling down the house. Right from the earliest verses of 1 Corinthians he has been dealing with divisions, cliques and parties in the church. People were making too much of him and Peter and Apollos and forming separate parties (see 3:3, 4; 1:11, 12), but only

one building should rise up on the one Foundation (v. 11). It is a desperate thing to pull down any of that building by falling out with each other – whatever the cause.

DAY 4
Read 2 Corinthians 6:14-18

Separate from all uncleanness
Suppose we had the visible presence of the Lord Jesus with us, how very careful we would be of the way we lived, the places we frequented, the books we read, the people we took as our friends, the interests we allowed to absorb us.

He is with us. He lives in His temple and we are the temple.

DAY 5
Read Jeremiah 7:9-11

Going out a different person
What is a robbers' den? It is a place to which robbers retire for safety and from which they emerge every bit as wicked and unreformed as they went in. Jeremiah saw people going into the temple which they prized so highly, participating there in the worship and then going home unreformed, with neither their past sins confessed and forgiven nor with their intended sins forsaken. Yet the Lord intended His house to be both these things: a place of forgiveness and of new commitment to lead a different life. This applies, too, to us as the Lord's temple today.

DAY 6
Read Isaiah 56:7b and Mark 11:15-17

The House of Prayer
Isaiah expressed the Lord's desire – a 'house of prayer' – and, seven hundred years later, the Lord Jesus reaffirmed

that this is what He wants. We may, of course, allow the word 'prayer' to cover the whole field of our individual and corporate life before God: praise and worship, thanksgiving, confession, intercession. When He entered Jerusalem this is what the Lord wanted to find, a people using God's house as God intended it. They, however, were turning it to their own commercial advantage instead of putting first what He longed for. How would the Lord Jesus react to us, His holy temple? Would He find that one thing which above all others He seeks and desires to find? Are we 'a house of prayer'?

DIAGRAM

Numbers 2

At the entrance to the Tent of Meeting ... I will meet with the children of Israel and the place will be consecrated by my glory.

I will dwell among the children of Israel and be their God. They will know that I am the Lord their God who brought them out of Egypt so that I might dwell among them. (Exod. 29:42-46)

What agreement is there between the temple of God and idols? For we are the temple of the living God. As God has said: I will live with them and walk among them, and

I will be their God and they will be my people. Therefore, come out ... and be separate. Touch no unclean thing and I will receive you. I will be a Father to you and you will be my sons and daughters, says the Lord Almighty. (2 Cor. 6:16-18, NIV)

Do you not know that you yourselves are God's temple and that God's Spirit lives in you? If anyone destroys God's temple, God will destroy him; for God's temple is holy, and you are that temple. (1 Cor. 3:16-17)

Will you steal and murder, commit adultery and perjury ... and follow others gods ... and then come and stand before me in this house ... and say, "We are safe" – safe to do all these detestable things? Has this house which bears my name become a den of robbers to you? (Jer. 7:9-11)

My house will be called a house of prayer. (Isa. 56:7)

Jesus entered the temple and began driving out those who were buying and selling there. He overturned the tables of the money-changers and the benches of those selling doves, and would not allow anyone to carry merchandise through the temple courts. And as he was teaching them, He said: My house will be called a house of prayer. (Mark 11:15-17)

The Story of Gideon in Seven Daily Portions

If you can make the time, read each portion in full. Otherwise, skim through the note and read the key verse.

DAY 1
Judges 6:1-10

The judgment of God on His sinful people (v. 1). Their land was devastated (v. 2). They were constantly harassed (v. 3). They were impoverished (vv. 4, 5). But they prayed (v. 6), and the Lord responded by calling them back to hear His Word (vv. 7-10).

Key Verse:

It was all their own fault but prayer was still the solution. (6:7)

DAY 2
Judges 6:11-27

The Angel of the Lord (an Old Testament 'preview' of Jesus) called an astonished Gideon to be the deliverer

(vv. 12-14), and promised His divine presence as all Gideon needed (vv. 15-16). Gideon said 'yes' by making an offering to the Lord (vv. 17-21). Gideon was assured that he had peace with God (vv. 22-23) and 'took his stand' by demolishing the altar of Baal (vv. 25-27).

Key Verse:

And the Lord said to him, 'Surely I will be with you'. (6:16)

DAY 3
Judges 6:28-40

When Gideon was publicly challenged for demolishing the altar, his father rescued him (v. 28-32), and the Lord too came to him in power (v. 34). Gideon began to gather his army (v. 35), and sought a sign from the Lord that he was acting in the right way (vv. 36-40).

Key Verse:

Literally, 'the Spirit ... put Gideon on (like a garment).'(6:34)

DAY 4
Judges 7:1-15

To Gideon's surprise, his great army of 32,000 was reduced by the Lord to 300 (vv. 1-6), with the promise that by them the Lord would save His people (v. 7). Gideon needed reassurance and the Lord gave it to him in a very remarkable way (vv. 8-15).

Key Verse:

God's work must be done God's way. (7:7)

DAY 5
Judges 7:16-25

Gideon's 300 men came unscathed through the battle (see 8:4) because the Lord intervened (v. 22) by making the Midianites, etc., attack each other. Other tribes joined Gideon's army (vv. 23-24) and Midianite power was cracked (v. 25).

Key Verse:

The Battle is the Lord's. (7:22)

DAY 6
Judges 8:1-21

Not all those who should have supported Gideon did so (vv. 4-9) – and paid the price (vv. 15-17). But as for Midian, victory was complete (vv. 18-21). Gideon was a 'complex character' – peacemaker (vv. 1-3), cruel avenger (vv. 12-17) , implacable enemy (vv. 18-21). A 'mixed-up kid' like the rest of us.

Key Verse:

The Lord must increase and 'I' must decrease. (8:3)

DAY 7
Judges 8:22-35

What sadness. Gideon the great failure! The lure of gold (vv. 24-26), leaving truth for error (v. 27), leading his people astray (v. 27), only limited success (v. 28), a lax old age (vv. 29-32), no lasting influence (vv. 33-35).

Key Verse:

At the end, self-enrichment, not God's glory, won the day. (8:24)

Appendix 7

Isaiah's Portrait of the Messiah

1. THE KING

Isaiah 1–37 is set in the times of Kings Ahaz and Hezekiah (735-700 B.C.). Against the background of Ahaz' failure, Isaiah depicts the coming perfect King.

DAY 1
Read Isaiah 2:2-4

According to 1:21, 26, the once-faithful city can look forward to its beginning coming back again – that is, the days of David. Isaiah is not forecasting any earthly Jerusalem but the heavenly city to which we who believe in Jesus now belong (Heb. 12:22-24) and which we also expect (Rev. 21:2, 3). It is the city (v. 3) where the Word of God is at the centre and is magnetic, the city to which all may come, and where peace prevails.

DAY 2
Read Isaiah 9:6-7

The Messiah is one to whom nothing is impossible ('wonderful'), the fount of truth ('counsellor'), God Himself come in power ('mighty God'), eternally tenderly caring for His family ('everlasting Father'), the source, giver and maintainer of peace ('Prince of peace'). All fulfilled in Jesus.

2. THE SERVANT OF THE LORD
King Hezekiah was given a promise of deliverance from Babylon (38:6), but chose rather deliverance by making an alliance (39:1-2). To refuse to believe the Lord's promises is one of the greatest of all sins. Against this background Isaiah foresaw the coming of a Saviour from sin.

DAY 3
Read Isaiah 49:5-6

In a way that would be fulfilled to the full in Jesus, the Lord's Servant is prepared from birth for his task. He will bring to the Lord both those who would already profess to know Him and also a worldwide people, all coming together in what Paul will call 'the Israel of God' (Gal. 6:16). The Servant brings light and salvation to the whole world.

DAY 4
Read Isaiah 50:4-5

The Servant exercises a uniformly helpful ministry – the 'word in season' – to people (v. 4a), and total obedience to the Lord (v. 5). The source of these characteristics was a sustained practice of starting the day with the Lord, to hear His Word (v. 4b).

DAY 5
Read Isaiah 53:4-6

Here is the great work of salvation. In verse 5, 'for' is literally 'because of'. Our transgressions were the cause of His sufferings. He took our place; paid the penalty due to us. In verse 6, note something true of all, something true of each, and something true of the Lord.

3. THE CONQUEROR
In chapters 56–66, the Lord's people, in all our inadequacy, are seen in the setting of a hostile, uncongenial world. The great Conqueror will come to rescue us and to deal finally with all His foes.

DAY 6
Read Isaiah 61:1-3 (with Luke 4:17-21)

In verses 1-2a, Isaiah notes seven things the Messiah will do (and which Jesus has done and will do). Pick them out, and ask how far we are experiencing the benefits of His activity.

DAY 7
Read Isaiah 63:1-6

Here is the Second Coming of Jesus (see 2 Thess. 1:7-10). In verse 1, 'Edom' typifies the whole hostile world. The work of both vengeance and salvation is something the Messiah does by Himself: He alone can save; He alone can judge. And this day is coming when our Lord returns.

Appendix **8**

Seven Daily Readings in Isaiah

In speaking of His own coming, Jesus foretold many troubles ahead for the Church but said, 'when you see these things (the troubles) begin ... then look up, lift up your heads for your redemption draws near' (Luke 21:28). This could well be a motto for the whole book of Isaiah: whenever he sees darkness ahead – defeat, enslavement, suffering, even suffering deserved because of sin – he allows the light of a great and sure Hope to shine, a Hope on which God's people can rest in faith while the trouble lasts.

DAY 1
Isaiah 5:1-7, 30

Trouble ahead
In chapters 1–5, Isaiah provides a sort of preface to his book: he shows what things were like when he was called

to be a prophet and began his work. Chapter 5 is the climax: he shows in a story how God had done absolutely everything for His people (vv. 1-2a) but look what He got in return (vv. 2b-4). Things can get no darker than when the Lord seems to have nothing more that even He can do. No wonder the chapter ends with total darkness (v. 30)!

DAY 2
Isaiah 6:1-8

Light in darkness
Isaiah discovered in experience that the Lord could save him from his sin – and (v. 5) his sin and his people's sin was the same: as the light shone on him so he knew there was hope for them too. Isaiah saw the Lord in His holiness (vv. 1-3), himself in his sinfulness and exclusion (vv. 4-5), the provision made by God for forgiveness of sins (vv. 6-7) and finally the Lord again, this time close enough to speak to.

DAY 3
Isaiah 7:1-9

Trouble ahead
King Ahaz was faced by a threat of invasion and was terrified (vv. 1-2). But he began to prepare the city for siege, examining the water supply (v. 3). Isaiah had a better recipe for security – Do nothing (v. 4) – literally 'See that you keep still', because the Lord promises it will not happen (v. 7). But if Ahaz will not believe the promise he will not continue (v. 9) – and, as a matter of fact, Ahaz did not believe, and the country entered the darkness of domination by the Assyrians.

DAY 4
Isaiah 9:1-7

Light in darkness
Beyond the darkness a great light shines. The coming blessings of God are worth waiting for: the joy of entering into a victory that has been won (v. 3), deliverance from oppression (v. 4), the end of the enemy (v. 5) – and all due to the birth of a child whose four names tell us in turn that He is full of wisdom for our guidance; He is truly God; He is ever fatherly in His care and concern; He brings and maintains peace.

DAY 5
Isaiah 38:1-6; 39:1-6

Trouble ahead
The Lord made a personal promise to Hezekiah of recovery (v. 5) and added a further promise that He would keep Jerusalem safe from Assyria. Both these promises were confirmed by a remarkable sign (vv. 7-8). Nothing could be plainer: the safety of the city was secured simply by believing the promise! But Hezekiah turned from the way of simple faith (39:1-2) by trying to form a military alliance with the rebel power of Babylon. Only the doom of captivity in Babylon could now follow.

DAY 6
Isaiah 40:1-2; 53:1-12

Light in darkness
No sooner has the Lord used Isaiah to predict doom than He sends him to proclaim comfort (40:1) and the forgiveness of their sins (v. 2). This work of dealing with

their sins was to be performed by the Servant of the Lord (52:13) who would be 'the Lord's arm' (53:1) – the Lord Himself come to save; He would grow as a man among men (53:2-3) and would die in our place (vv. 4-6, 8, 10-12).

DAY 7
Isaiah 56:1, etc.

Trouble ahead, Light in darkness
Patience is called for to wait for the great salvation (56:1) and to be obedient (56:2) to God's Word. Especially as circumstances are so difficult and sin so strong (59:9-15). But the Lord has committed Himself to come to overthrow His people's foes and to save them (59:16-20) to conquer and to comfort (40:1-6).

Appendix 9

A Seven-Day Reading Scheme on Malachi

DAY 1
Malachi 1:1-5

Malachi found his people bothered about the love of God: it somehow did not always seem clear that He did, in fact love them. In reply, Malachi urges them to look back (vv. 2b-3a) to the basic fact of the Lord's choice of Jacob rather than Esau (Gen. 25:23; Rom. 9:10-13), to look around (v. 3b) at the evidence of Esau's present experience and to look forward (vv. 4-5) to the outcome which would prove the Lord's love to them. So we can look back to what God has done for us in Jesus, around to the many evidences of His present love and forward to heaven.

DAY 2
Malachi 1:6-14

Do we try to get our religion on the cheap? Verses 6a and 8b offer illustrations of what Malachi has in mind: behaving towards God in ways we would never dream of towards earthly superiors! In verses 6b, 7 and 8a, he spells this out in the terms of his own day when animal sacrifice was the practice. If folk go on like this, then (vv. 9-11) the Lord will not have it and will find His true worshippers elsewhere! Instead of His blessing we could earn only His curse (vv. 12-14).

DAY 3
Malachi 2:1-9

These verses are addressed specially to leaders of the Church but all can learn the lessons inasmuch as we all have responsibilities to God for others. Verses 1-3: if the Church does not put God first, it loses the ability to be a blessing to people.

Verses 4-9: what is a priest for? To walk with God in deep reverence for His name (i.e. the revelation which He has given of Himself, (vv. 4-5); to teach people God's truth and turn them from any and every wickedness of life – i.e. to inform and reform (vv. 6-7). What a sad record of failure in verses 8-9.

DAY 4
Malachi 2:10-16

Sins against marriage are the special object of God's hatred. In verses 10-12, Malachi rebukes people for marrying those who do not acknowledge and worship the Lord; verse 13 shows the power of sin to stand between us and God, to create a barrier and to prevent us from enjoying the privilege of answered prayer. Verses 14-16 are very straight in their meaning though some parts are hard to explain in detail: the Lord hates divorce.

DAY 5
Malachi 2:17–3:6

We must often wonder today what is happening to moral values. So did people in Malachi's day! Is it possible to say any longer what is good and what is bad? Does God indeed care? Verse 17 is a cynical comment: plainly wicked people get on very well – does God then approve of them? Is He concerned about good and evil? Malachi calls people to look forward. God is coming to them and when He does, He will show Himself to be a purifier and concerned with moral values (as indeed happened when Jesus came, did it not?) (vv. 1-3). He is still the God of the Ten Commandments (vv. 4-6).

DAY 6
Malachi 3:7-17

Here is another section about religion on the cheap. In 1:6-8, it was a matter of trying to fob God off with less than the best; here (vv. 7-8) it is a matter of trying to give God less than the whole of His requirement. But what blessings will be poured on those who hold nothing back from God of that which He asks (vv. 9-10)! In verses 13-17, the Lord recognises that those who want to be faithful to Him have a hard world to live in but He urges the benefits of fellowship (v. 16), assures them that He has them in mind and in His book (v. 16b) and will keep them ever safe (v. 17).

DAY 7
Malachi 3:18–4:6

The day of the Lord is coming (for us, the Return of our Lord Jesus Christ): for some (4:1), a day of disaster; for others (4:2-3), of healing, liberty and victory over every foe. What folk fall into each group? In the waiting time (vv. 4-6), we are called to walk with God in obedience to His law.

Appendix 10

God Our Father:
A Thought for Five Days

Monday

How great the Father is, and how gracious!
The Father is Lord of heaven and earth (Matt. 11:25);
He is supremely great (John 14:28). He is also supremely
loving (John 3:16). The Son came to us from the
Father (John 16:28) and it is through the working of
the Father's power that we come to Jesus (John 6:44).
We can come right into the Father's presence in prayer
(John 15:16).

Other verses to look up, if time allows: Matthew 11:26;
John 14:16; 16:23; John 4:21, 23; John 14:6, 7, 9; 16:27.

Tuesday

The Father is only known through the Son
John 1:18 gives a lovely picture of closeness and intimacy between Father and the Son. Jesus, God's Son, came to share His secrets with us. Only through Jesus can we come to the Father (John 14:6) and know Him as He is (John 14:9). The Father loves those who love Jesus (John 16:27).

Other verses to look up, if time allows: John 16:28; John 16:15; Luke 11:13; John 12:50.

Wednesday

'My Father': Jesus reveals His Father to us
In the Gospels, Jesus spoke nearly fifty times of 'My Father': in these verses, John 1:18 is fulfilled – the Son shares with us the secrets only He knows about the Father. The Father answers prayer (Matt. 18:19), loves those who love His Son (John 14:21), is glorified when we bear much fruit (John 15:8). The Father gave His son the cup of suffering to drink (Matt. 26:39, 41; John 18:11) and it is to the Father's house we go after death (John 14:2).

Other verses to look up, if time allows: Matthew 7:21; 18:35; 25:34; Luke 2:49; 24:49; John 6:32; John 10:17, 18, 28, 29.

Thursday

'Your Father': Jesus speaks of His Father as our Father
We are called to be like our Father (Matt. 5:45, 48). Our Father knows our needs (Matt. 6:8, 32) and gives good things in answer to prayer (Matt. 7:11). He is glorified when we live according to His will (Matt. 5:16) and delights to give us His kingdom (Luke 12:32).

Other verses to look up, if time allows: Luke 6:36; Matthew 6:1; Matthew 6:26; 10:29; Luke 12:30; Matthew 13:43.

Friday

'Thy Father': the Father of Jesus is the Father of each believer in Jesus
Jesus only speaks three times of 'Thy Father': Matthew 6:4, 6, 18. These verses sum up and apply the teaching of Matthew 6:1 – we are to live our lives under the Father's eye and with the intention to please Him. There are three aspects of this life: it reaches out to help the needy (vv. 2-4), reaches upwards to the Father in prayer (vv. 6-15), and reaches inwards, into our own lives, as we express our commitment to the Father in self-sacrifice (vv. 16-18). We can deliberately set out to receive the 'rewards' the Father offers by our relationships to others in terms of help and care; our life of secret prayer; and our disciplined attitude towards ourselves.

It is our joy to know the Father: A living relationship

Luke 11:2	When you pray, say, Our Father ...
Luke 11:5	Which of you shall have a friend
Luke 11:11	If a son shall ask ... a father
Luke 11:13	How much more shall your Father give ...
John 16:26, 27	In that day you shall ask in my name: and I say not unto you that I will pray the Father for you, for the Father Himself loves you ...

Even the most difficult experiences of life happen within the Father's care: A demanding Trust

John 18:11   Jesus said to Peter, Put up your sword into the sheath: the cup which my Father has given me, shall I not drink it?

We will spend eternity in the Father's house: A glorious Expectation

John 14:2, 3   In my Father's house are many mansions ... I go to prepare a place for you ... that where I am, there you may be also.

No one can pluck us out of the Father's hand: A secure Rest

John 10:27-30   My sheep hear my voice and I know them and they follow me: and I give unto them eternal life; and they shall never perish, neither shall anyone pluck them out of my hand. My Father who gave them to me is greater than all: and no one is able to pluck them out of my FATHER's hand. I and my Father are one.

Also available from Dr Motyer ...

Isaiah by the Day
A New Devotional Translation

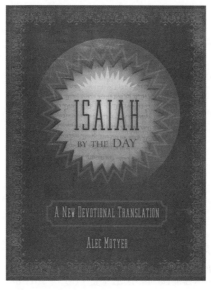

As a man who loves the Word of God, Alec Motyer presents these daily devotionals from Isaiah. For him, daily devotion is not a mere habit but a real desire to be transformed by the challenging word of Isaiah. These devotionals reassure us that the Lord can restore what sin has robbed us of. These daily devotionals are birthed from a lifetime of study on the prophecy of Isaiah. Day by day you will be provided with passages from Isaiah and an opportunity to explore the passage further. Take time to acquaint yourself with these passages from God's Word and treasure them in your heart.

ISBN 978-1-84550-654-4

Life 2: The Sequel

What happens when you die?

Many ideas of what happens at the end of this life have entered mainstream public thought. In the postmodern mindset, all are equally valid and all are equally possible – but are they all equally thought through? That is what acclaimed biblical scholar, Alec Motyer, sets out to do in this accessible and challenging investigation.

The nine chapters are clearly set out to help you find the answers biblically. For example: In chapter 3 the Doctrine of Universalism is explored under topics, e.g., Scriptural support, defining God as love, the Cross & human freedom. The arguments are put forward from Scripture so you've no excuses! Are you certain that death is the end – or is there a *Life 2: The Sequel?*

ISBN 978-1-84550-343-7

Roots

Let the Old Testament Speak

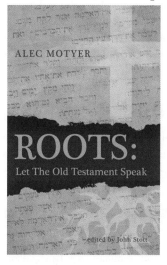

There are questions that Alec Motyer, a lifelong lover of the Old Testament, seeks to answer, starting with the conviction that Jesus is the fulfilment of the Old Testament Scripture. This is for the Christian who wants to know what the Old Testament has to do with the New Testament and why the Christian should read it.

His [Motyer's] mastery of the Hebrew text, his knowledge of the Old Testament background, and his conviction that Jesus Christ is the fulfilment of the law and prophets together give him a rare ability to paint the big picture and to tell the 'story within the story' of the Old Testament.

John Stott (1921-2011)
Rector Emeritus, All Souls Church, Langham Place, London

ISBN 978-1-84550-506-6

Christian Focus Publications

Our mission statement –

STAYING FAITHFUL

In dependence upon God we seek to impact the world through literature faithful to His infallible Word, the Bible. Our aim is to ensure that the Lord Jesus Christ is presented as the only hope to obtain forgiveness of sin, live a useful life and look forward to heaven with Him.

Our books are published in four imprints:

CHRISTIAN
FOCUS

Popular works including biographies, commentaries, basic doctrine and Christian living.

CHRISTIAN
HERITAGE

Books representing some of the best material from the rich heritage of the church.

MENTOR

Books written at a level suitable for Bible College and seminary students, pastors, and other serious readers. The imprint includes commentaries, doctrinal studies, examination of current issues and church history.

CF4•K

Children's books for quality Bible teaching and for all age groups: Sunday school curriculum, puzzle and activity books; personal and family devotional titles, biographies and inspirational stories – Because you are never too young to know Jesus!

Christian Focus Publications Ltd,
Geanies House, Fearn, Ross-shire,
IV20 1TW, Scotland, United Kingdom.
www.christianfocus.com